"Every chapter explodes with pure awesomeness. You will laugh. You will cry. And you will love Jesus more. I promise."

—DERWIN L. GRAY, LEAD PASTOR, TRANSFORMATION CHURCH; AUTHOR, *Limitless Lifes*

"Naeem's story is really a story of God's passionate and relentless pursuit of people. Reading it will remind you that God is in your story, in your life, drawing you closer to him."

—MARK BATTERSON, LEAD PASTOR, NATIONAL COMMUNITY CHURCH; *New York Times* BESTSELLING AUTHOR, *The Circle Maker*

"Every page of Naeem's story is a reminder that—no matter what's going on in your life—you can discover and sustain a hope that transcends your current circumstances."

—PETE WILSON, LEAD PASTOR, CROSS POINT CHURCH; AUTHOR, *Plan B* AND *Let Hope In*

"My friend Naeem is a trophy of God's grace. In this book, you'll experience his remarkable story in a way that will illuminate the path of your spiritual journey as well."

—STEVEN FURTICK, LEAD PASTOR, ELEVATION CHURCH; *New York Times* BESTSELLING AUTHOR, *Sun Stand Still*

"Ridiculously funny, witty, and certain to keep your attention. Naeem's story is mind blowing, a real testimony to the power of God redeeming a new generation."

—PETER HAAS, LEAD PASTOR, SUBSTANCE CHURCH; AUTHOR, *Pharisectomy*

"With crosscultural candor, unexpected humor, and his passionate love for Jesus, Naeem Fazal shares an inspiring epic adventure of faith in Ex-Muslim. His perspective not only provides insight into the Islamic culture, but also reveals the power of the Gospel to transcend any barrier, label, or expectation."

—CHRIS HODGES, SENIOR PASTOR, CHURCH OF
THE HIGHLANDS; AUTHOR, *Fresh Air*

"Don't let *Ex-Muslim* fool you into thinking it's just a personal story. It is beyond rich and layered in a much larger and deeper message—one the church so badly needs to hear."

—ROBYN AFRIK, SPEAKER, AUTHOR, AND CEO OF AFRIK ADVANTAGE

"*Ex-Muslim* will encourage you to rethink whether your relationship with God is cultural and performance-based, or is based on embracing the grace and kindness of God."

—RICK BEZET, FOUNDER AND LEAD PASTOR, NEW LIFE
CHURCH IN CENTRAL ARKANSAS; AUTHOR, *BE REAL*

"Naeem's redemptive story is proof that God can do anything in our lives. No matter where we have been or our current circumstances, God can use us to make a difference in our world. This is a must-read!"

—CASEY GRAHAM, FOUNDER, THE ROCKET COMPANY

"Naeem Fazal is one of the most dynamic, Christ-centered, voices of his generation; and after reading *Ex-Muslim*, you'll know why."

DR. MARK DEYMAZ, FOUNDING PASTOR, MOSAIC
CHURCH OF CENTRAL ARKANSAS; AUTHOR,
Building a Healthy Multi-ethnic Church

"Naeem's life illustrates the strength and faithfulness of God and his story reflects God's love and mercy."

PASTOR MICHAEL MORRIS (MOOSE), SEACOAST CHURCH

"Naeem's modern-day encounter with Jesus is like reading about the apostle Paul's run-in with Jesus over two thousand years ago. You'll be captivated from the first page."

"The first time I heard Naeem tell his story, it startled me and spurred me on to greater faith in Jesus. *Ex-Muslim* will give you a loving push to let God do more than you could ask or imagine in your daily life."

"This story will ignite passion, fervor, and exuberance with expectancy."

Ex-Muslim

Ex-Muslim

How One Daring Prayer
to Jesus Changed a
Life Forever

NAEEM FAZAL

with KITTI MURRAY

NELSON
BOOKS

An Imprint of Thomas Nelson

Published in Nashville, Tennessee, by Nelson Books, an imprint of Thomas Nelson. Nelson Books and Thomas Nelson are registered trademarks of HarperCollins Christian Publishing, Inc.

Published in association with the literary agency of Mark Sweeney & Associates, Bonita Springs, Florida 34135

Thomas Nelson, Inc., titles may be purchased in bulk for educational, business, fund-raising, or sales promotional use. For information, please e-mail SpecialMarkets@ThomasNelson.com.

All Scripture references, unless otherwise noted, are from THE ENGLISH STANDARD VERSION. © 2001 by Crossway Bibles, a division of Good News Publishers. Scripture references marked HCSB are from the HOLMAN CHRISTIAN STANDARD BIBLE. © 1999, 2000, 2002, 2003 by Broadman and Holman Publishers. All rights reserved. Scripture references marked MSG are from *The Message* by Eugene H. Peterson. © 1993, 1994, 1995, 1996, 2000. Used by permission of NavPress Publishing Group. All rights reserved. Scripture references marked NIRV are from Holy Bible, NEW INTERNATIONAL READER'S VERSION®. Copyright © 1996, 1998 Biblica. All rights reserved throughout the world. Used by permission of Biblica. Scripture references marked NIV are from *HOLY BIBLE*: NEW INTERNATIONAL VERSION®. © 1973, 1978, 1984, 2011 by Biblica, Inc™ Used by permission of Zondervan Publishing House. All rights reserved. Scripture references marked NLT are from *Holy Bible*, New Living Translation. © 1996. Used by permission of Tyndale House Publishers, Inc., Wheaton, Illinois 60189. All rights reserved. Scripture references marked NASB are from New America Standard Bible®. © The Lockman Foundation 1960, 1962, 1963, 1968, 1971, 1972, 1973, 1975, 1977. Used by permission.

The Library of Congress Cataloging-in-Publication Data
is on file with the Library of Congress.

ISBN-13: 978-1-40020-6-070

Printed in the United States of America

14 15 16 17 18 RRD 6 5 4 3 2 1

*To my parents, Balques Akhtar and
Mohammed Fazal Rahim Ali.*

*Thank you for courageously allowing me to
become the person I was created to be.*

CONTENTS

CONTENTS

Author's Note

Sometimes I wish I wasn't an Ex-Muslim. I love Muslims. I love their hospitality, their culture, and their authenticity. It saddens me that following Jesus sometimes creates distance between me and the people I feel closest to. I wish I could tell them that being Ex-Muslim in no way makes me Anti-Muslim. I simply met Jesus, and now I cannot deny him.

FOREWORD

I'VE HAD THE GREAT PRIVILEGE of knowing Naeem Fazal for nearly a decade. We have journeyed together on a great quest and through it have shared life and friendship together. I love Naeem as a brother and celebrate that his life has been transformed by the undeniable hand of God on his life.

Those of us at Mosaic in Los Angeles felt honored when Naeem asked to partner with us and launched a Mosaic in Charlotte. We were inspired by his story and knew that his was a story that would help many find their way to the God of the Scriptures.

Over the years I have had the opportunity to travel into, and share life with, the people of Pakistan, Syria, Lebanon, Egypt, and Turkey. I have loved the Middle East and have found kindred spirits everywhere I have gone. From each of these countries I have met Muslims who are gracious, kind, hospitable, and on sincere journeys of faith. There is much that we share together. There is great truth between us. The conflict of the Middle East is a tragic conflict among brothers. I am convinced Naeem's story is a way toward peace. It is the way of Jesus that can bring healing to a troubled land.

Both Christians and Muslims acknowledge the words of Jesus as sacred. Naeem's is a story of hope. In his story there is the promise of a future where enemies become friends, and rediscover that we were brothers all along.

I love that Naeem is a reminder that we can all become a part of a bigger story—a better story. Our paths can begin from such divergent beginnings and still lead us straight to Jesus. God reveals himself to one through a conversation; to another through a dream. It is always a miracle.

Naeem most accurately was a devout Muslim to whom God revealed himself undeniably. He did not become a Christian and then met Jesus, nor did he come to believe in Jesus and then become a Christian. Naeem was a Muslim whose life was invaded by the person of Jesus. His story to me is not about an ex-Muslim. Naeem is a Muslim who met Jesus.

This is a beautiful story that reminds us that God is everywhere, speaking to all of us, calling us to himself. Thank you, Naeem, for stretching our faith and challenging our western presupposition about how God works.

Peter told us in the Scriptures that this would happen—that old men would dream dreams and young men would have visions.

Naeem, your faith began with a vision, may it end with the realization of your great dreams.

May all who read the pages of this book be filled with dreams and visions inspired by the God of Abraham, Isaac, and Jacob.

Shalom,
Erwin Raphael McManus
Mosaic, Los Angeles, CA

ONE

COME ON DOWN

If you wish for light, be ready to receive light.
—MATHNAWI I

THE OFFICIAL REASON FOR MY first trip to the United States was to visit my older brother. Mahmood was then a student at the College of Charleston, a fact that gave my family just cause to apply for travel visas. The application for my entire family—my mom, dad, two sisters, younger brother, and me—was a ruse to get me, just me, out of Kuwait. So I came to visit and, my family hoped, to stay put for the rest of my life. At the time, Kuwait was still reeling from the aftershocks of the Gulf War, and I was the next in line, after my brother, to escape. I'll never forget my dad's last words to me: "*Naeem beta vapus nahi ana, Tumhare liya ab yahan kuch nahi hai.* (Naeem, don't come back. There is nothing left for you here.)"

I was excited to see Moody (the name we all called Mahmood). But I had concerns too. My brother had been in the States for almost four years, and in that time he'd changed.

1

He'd changed so dramatically that the last time I saw him I had pinned him against a wall and threatened to kill him. During the first week of his most recent visit home to Kuwait he'd taken me aside to say he had, as he put it, "become a Christian." Now, here in the United States, that phrase is almost as common in some regions as "I'm a Lakers fan," but in Kuwait, where Islam is not only our religion but our nationality—our very identity—the only possible response to such a claim is outrage. Becoming a Christian meant rejecting your heritage. It was an insult. Worse, it was treason. Any Muslim who converted to Christianity was considered a *kafir,* an infidel. Add to all this my teenage need for equilibrium in my environment, for everyone I loved to just stick with the status quo, and Moody's announcement detonated in my chest like the IEDs that dotted our countryside during the war. In my mind, he had ruined our family, and—maybe even worse—ruined my chances of going to the United States. My parents would never let me go if this *sacrilege* is what happened over there. I could never actually hurt my brother physically, but I did end our relationship. I quit sharing my life with him. And I began to distrust him. So the subject was closed; we didn't go there anymore.

Before cutting him off and basically refusing to acknowledge his presence for the rest of his visit home, I warned Mahmood that he had better not tell anyone else his news. I think the vehemence of my response surprised him, so he took my demand seriously. He backed off, and he didn't tell anyone else. He even took off the cross he'd been wearing under his shirt. I thought to myself, *Good. I've shut him up.*

I was a little smug about that. I'd handled my oldest brother—the brother who, according to custom, was the favored son in our family. The one who was born with the light skin that was so desirable to Pakistani families, while I, the second born, was as dark as our *kahawa* (coffee). The good student who, unlike me—the screwup—made good grades and got into an American college. The good Muslim who won Qu'ran recitation contests. The family member who'd escaped the hell the rest of us had lived through during the Gulf War. I arrived in Charleston determined to communicate in no uncertain terms that my brother could go through his "Christian phase" all he wanted, but I was going to do my own thing. *Introduce me to girls and the good life, but don't introduce me to your Jesus. Point me in the right direction, Moody, but then get out of my way.*

It turns out I needed my brother's help far more than I needed him to stay away from me. I didn't know a soul in Charleston. My English was good, but nothing like the slow, folksy version I heard here. Without his social patronage I would have been incredibly lonely. He was a college student after all. And where else was I going to find the blonde American women I'd heard all about?

The first Tuesday I was in Charleston, Mahmood took me to a meeting of a group called Fellowship of Christian Athletes (FCA). Sure enough, there were blonde girls there—lots of them—which was why I kept going every Tuesday even though I sat in the back and made fun of all those crazy Christians who, by the way, weren't athletes at all. Go figure. I stayed on the periphery and observed, which can be loosely translated "checked out the girls." But the gospel is alive, and it has a way of sliding under barriers. I didn't listen, but somehow I heard. I sat on the outside looking in at those meetings, my outside self saying, *Jesus, yeah, yeah . . . Give me a clean heart. Sure.* But a door in my soul began to open so imperceptibly that I didn't even see the thin beam of light slipping through.

Mahmood's friends talked to me about Jesus. My brother kept quiet and let them do the talking. During conversations with my brother, I tried to talk to him about all the stuff I planned to do once I got this living-in-America thing figured out. I thought if I filled his imagination with what was important to me—my big dreams and goals—he wouldn't bother me with what was important to him. Eventually I asked Mahmood a question or two about Christianity. Or, rather, I goaded him.

One night, after hanging out with a bunch of FCA people at a place called Aunt Fannie's, we were walking back to our apartment. Our discussion devolved into an argument.

"You know, Moody, this idea that God is personal is ridiculous. There's no way that can be true," I said pompously. I thought I'd stuck a barb straight into the one major flaw of the gospel. Personal God? Any good Muslim knew Allah was far removed from us and to be feared. He was the Almighty. How could my brother believe in such a blasphemous thing as a personal God? He should know the natural and the supernatural never connect in Muslim theology.

"What do you mean it can't be true?"

"If what you say about Jesus is true," I said, again thinking I had him backed into a corner, "then why doesn't he come on down here and prove it?"

I pointed to a bush that seemed conveniently placed along our path and, chuckling at my own cleverness, I said, "Why doesn't your Jesus zap this bush and make it burn? If he's so big and bad, why doesn't he come down and *reveal himself to me personally* right now," I mimicked the way some of Mahmood's Christian friends talked and prayed that God would "come on down."

To my surprise my brother didn't seem at all daunted by my mockery. "He'll do it, Naeem. If you just ask him to, he'll do it. It might not be tonight, but he will."

"Whatever," I said, a little deflated because I didn't have an answer for a claim like that. Honestly, I was shocked by his confidence. It made me more curious than I wanted to admit.

One Tuesday night the FCA leaders showed a film about the Rapture, an interesting concept that baffles me to this day. Instead of derision, I responded with curiosity, nothing more. Still, mild interest is a far cry from outright scorn. Sometimes the miracles that happen in our hearts begin subtly like that.

The group ended the night with prayer the way they always did. And I prayed. The way I saw it, my brother had dared me to pray for God to "come down," to reveal himself in a personal way, whatever that meant. So it was time to make good on my promise. It's hard for me to refuse a dare, so I had no choice.

"Whoever you are, whoever is up there, if you're real, if what my idiot brother says about you is true, then why don't you show me?" I said out loud to God, not really sure it was prayer. And then I added, "I don't believe any of this, so you're going to have to prove it. I know I'm just talking to myself."

Instead of "Amen" I ended the prayer with "Whatever," or something like that. I prayed for the God I didn't believe in to come down and do what I thought he couldn't do.

And God heard.

Darkness

It was three nights later. After midnight, I was in my bed at my brother's apartment, closing the novel I'd been reading, dropping it on the table beside me, stretching that final, get-settled-for-the-night stretch. But instead of drifting off to sleep, I was suddenly wide awake. I don't know if being a Muslim made me more vulnerable or less vulnerable to what happened next.

In Muslim culture, we don't dwell on the "dark side." There is no focus on demons or Satan. In fact, it seems as if most Muslims fear God more than Satan. And so when the room grew unnaturally dark and the atmosphere became—well, the only word for it is *evil*—I had absolutely no clue what was happening. I just know that it felt weird. And then, quickly, terrifying. Something grabbed my shoulders and pinned me to my pillow. A presence of some kind sat on my legs, and I could not move. I began to scream, to swear, to cry out in hopes that my brother would hear and come to my rescue. I had no precedent for this. I'd just lived through the Gulf War with missile strikes and oil fires often only a block away from our home, but in that moment I was more petrified than I'd ever been in my short life. The room got darker, more alive, and I screamed louder.

The door creaked open, and I felt a momentary pulse of relief, thinking my brother was finally there. I looked up and saw an even larger, darker presence. It moved toward me, communicating with me in unspoken words, but I knew exactly what it was saying: *I'm going to kill you.* Unintelligible yet unmistakable language. Somewhere in my memory, I retrieved enough information to realize that these were demons. I thought at them, *I'm a Muslim; I don't believe in demons*, not that my unbelief seemed to matter one bit to them.

My next instinct was to pray, but to whom? Allah? Buddha? Oprah? Hello, anyone? Then I thought of Jesus. I'd prayed to him three nights before, and *this* was what I got? I began some impressive backpedaling, retracting my prayer as quickly as I could. Had I prayed all wrong? Was this my punishment for being so cavalier with Jesus? "I'm sorry," I groveled, "I didn't mean it, Jesus. I was stupid, Jesus!"

I meant it too. On some visceral level that I didn't understand at the time, I truly meant it. I genuinely cried out to Jesus *as if he were real*.

The being did not retreat; it suddenly disappeared. The weight on my body lifted and left. The room was still soaked in darkness, still felt malevolent, but I knew I was safe for the time being. I looked around for just a moment before jumping out of bed and doing what any self-respecting grown man would do. I ran to my brother's room, climbed in his bed, and, trembling like a little girl, woke him up.

Just Like in the Movies

Until that night, my stay in the States had been a boy's lark, more daydream than nightmare. Even so, my first day here, a scant month earlier, had been a little disappointing.

When I left Kuwait, I left a family divided by the hard decisions the war had caused us to make. I had not graduated from high school because my school building had been destroyed—every teenager's dream—as a parting gift of the Iraqi forces. In many respects I was running away from home, and running straight into the arms of freedom and the American dream. Of course I had no clue I would be battling literal demons within my first month here.

I was only eighteen, and my hopes and ambitions surely reflected my youth. What was I most excited about while preparing for a visit to this new land of opportunity—a visit I hoped would result in a permanent stay? Maybe you've already guessed: blondes. Specifically, blonde, blue-eyed girls. And where did my direct flight land me? In Miami, where everyone—and I mean everyone—looked exactly like me. At first I wondered if I'd landed in the wrong place, if Miami was a separate country. It's ironic, isn't it? Here I was the farthest away from home I'd ever been, and, on the surface, it sure looked like I fit right in. (I've been accused on YouTube of being a fake, not Middle Eastern at all, and certainly not a former Muslim. People think I'm Hispanic.)

I stayed with a cousin in Miami, and then in the predawn hours two weeks later I got on a bus bound for Charleston, South Carolina, where Mahmood lived. Kuwait is very small. You can probably travel its outer boundaries three whole times in two hours. I hadn't paid close attention to the arrival time stamped on my ticket, so I was the pesky passenger who walked up the aisle several times an hour and tapped the bus driver on the shoulder to ask, "Are we there yet?" After a few times, he shot me a nasty look and said, "It's in *South Carolina*, buddy," as if I should know how far away that is in Greyhound miles, or in any miles for that matter. I'll tell you how far away it is: seventeen and a half hours. My cousin apparently didn't know about express tickets, so he'd bought me one with stops in every major city and every obscure town between Miami and Charleston. Let's just say I saw the good, the bad, and the ugly of my new homeland on that trip.

We hadn't gone far before we stopped in Cocoa Beach. By that time I'd resigned myself to a longer journey than expected, so I decided to relax, take a walk around outside, and smoke a cigarette. As I lit up, I noticed the sky was turning from gray to pale pink. I ambled around to the back of the building thinking, *I can't believe I'm in the USA. I've made it. This is going to be an interesting life.* (I had no idea.) I walked back to the front of the bus station feeling more relaxed.

Until I noticed that my bus was gone.

I mean, the exhaust had already dissipated. No taillights receding on the flat Florida horizon. It was gone. I ran to the ticket window and blurted out, my accent becoming as thick as my panic, like it always does when I freak out, "Excuse me. Where's my bus?"

"Oh," the lady behind the glass answered, so nonchalantly that I felt a flicker of hope that there might not be a problem after all, "the bus is gone."

"It's coming back, right? Gone where? To refuel?"

"No, it's gone to Charleston."

"Are you kidding me?" I said. And then I said some other things I'd rather leave to your imagination.

The ticket agent didn't answer. It was a rhetorical question anyway. But then I started thinking rationally again, and I asked, "When is the next bus?"

"Uh, tomorrow. Twenty-four hours from now."

Unbelievable. I walked outside just as the sun, big and

glorious, peeked over the big, glorious Atlantic Ocean. But all I could think about was my seat on that bus and the things I'd left there: my passport, all my papers, everything I had. No sunrise could distract me from *that*. And then I saw the solution: a yellow car idling on the curb. Taxis in Kuwait City are either beige and white or orange, but I recognized it anyway, thanks to my extensive experience watching American movies. I knocked on the window, waking the driver, and motioned for him to roll his window down. I said, "Listen, I missed my bus, and I need you to take me to South Carolina."

When I left Kuwait, my father had insisted I keep eighty dollars or so in, of all places, my sock, so I pulled out the entire roll of smelly, damp cash and handed it to him. "It's all yours; just get me to South Carolina."

I don't think the cab drivers in Cocoa Beach get that kind of request every day. He looked at me like I was an alien, which, technically, I was. "*Where?*"

"Charleston, South Carolina," I said, and if I'd known more English idioms back then, I would have added, "And make it snappy."

Snappy didn't begin to express how desperately I needed transportation at that moment. I expected him to blow me off, but he seemed to understand. "Why? What happened?"

After a few sentences from me, he said, "All right, all right, let me see what I can do," and he walked inside the station to talk with the ticket agent.

I began to wonder if he was in there reporting me to somebody, but then he came out and said, "Okay, let's catch your bus."

He'd gotten a list of the next few bus stops on my route and wisely determined to save me the money and himself the hassle by getting me back on my bus instead of driving me all the way to South Carolina.

My mood shifted from desperation to exhilaration in sixty seconds flat. All I could think as we sped down the highway was, *This is just like the movies.* The next stop was a large hub with almost too many buses to count. I frantically looked around and couldn't find mine, so we sped to the next station. Several stops later, still no bus. And then there it was. (Cue the music.) Picture it: I saw the bus and the bus saw me. I ran for it, hopped on, and went to what I was sure was my seat. Empty.

By this point I was ready to swear in every language I know. A paralyzing dread settled over me. I'd lost everything. My last eighty dollars, my phone numbers, my contact information for anyone I could call in a crisis, everything I owned except the clothes on my back. I stepped out of the wrong bus, utterly defeated. And then, across the parking lot, I saw my bus driver. Or maybe I should call him my nemesis. *What's he doing on the wrong bus?* I thought. And then it hit me. *That's my bus.* I raced to it and climbed on. I ran to my seat and discovered all my belongings just as I'd left them.

I determined to never leave the bus again, no matter how badly I had to . . . you know . . . go, until I saw my brother's face on the platform in Charleston, South Carolina. I sat down to wait. *I can do this,* I thought. *God bless America.*

Face-to-Face

I was never happier to see my brother than the night I honestly but ignorantly cried out to Jesus to save my life. After I shook him awake, yelling "Moody! What the hell is going on?" and told him what had happened, he said something that made perfect sense.

"Maybe it was just a dream."

But I knew better. "Look at my shoulders," I said, my panic rising again at the memory, "the marks from . . . from whatever that was holding me down are still here. What's going on?"

I love my brother, but he clearly didn't know much about how to calm a trauma victim. For the next half hour he droned on and on about the gospel and the theology of demons and angels, until I grabbed his arm and said, "Moody, I have no idea what any of this means, but I do know I'm afraid for my *life*. Something out there wants to kill me. I can feel it."

He stopped and looked at me, examining my face for a moment. "You know, Naeem, I think you are on top of a hill."

Metaphors? Seriously, bro, you've got to be kidding me, I thought.

"Listen, Naeem," he said, more patiently than I felt the situation warranted, "you're on this hill, and you could fall either way. One side represents the world and all your ambitions. The other side represents God and his kingdom. I believe what is happening is the enemy of the spiritual side—Satan—is trying to scare you away from the right side of the mountain."

That kind of made sense to me, and I told Mahmood so. "But I'm really scared to death," I confessed.

And then my brother said the one thing that not only made sense, but also made a difference to my quaking soul that night. "You know, there is only one person who has authority over demons and angels."

"Who?" I asked, at once hopeful and afraid, because I knew I wasn't going to like the answer.

But right then I didn't care if it was Jesus Christ—the one who had ruined my relationship with my brother, the one who stood for dissonance and disunity in my family, the one who, if I were to follow him, would mean the betrayal of just about everything I had believed in until that moment.

Mahmood began to pray to Jesus on my behalf, for my salvation not just from demons but also from darkness into light, from death into life. He took me through a few verses in the book of Romans, ending with: "If you confess with your mouth that Jesus is Lord and believe in your heart that God raised him from the dead, you will be saved" (Rom. 10:9 NLT). He prayed for me to have a new life; then he asked me to repeat a prayer after him. I prayed with him, repenting from my sins and inviting Jesus into my life. I understood that this had to be authentic. I said, "Jesus, I don't even know you, so I can't truly claim to love you or say that you're my Lord. But if you will help me, I will give you my life."

And then I waited for it to happen. You know, peace and tranquility and an unconquerable sense of safety. But it didn't. With a final word, *amen*, it seemed to be over. Mahmood gave me a miniscule New Testament, one of those green fake-leather Gideon ones with the golden urn stamped on front. "I want you to go back in your room and read the book of John. We'll talk in the morning," he told me, dismissing me as if I were a middle school kid.

"Go back to my room? No way! Move over, dude, I'm spooning with you tonight."

"No, you're not. Just read the book of John and go to sleep."

"At least give me a bigger Bible so when I throw it I can do some damage," I pled after several more appeals to sleep in his bed.

But once again, he dared me, so I went back to my room.

I turned on every light in the room, plus the bathroom light. I sat on the bed, tucked the covers around my body like a hermetic seal, and started reading John in tiny print. But I couldn't concentrate, not when there were sounds everywhere. The bathroom creaked as if its tiles were shifting. When you're scared, everything is noisy—even the air. The window rattled. And pretty soon, I was just as rattled as before.

"Okay." I assessed my situation. "I'm a Muslim who just prayed to Jesus.

"But I don't *want* Jesus.

"I am a Christian now. I just got attacked by demons, and I don't even believe in demons. Why is this happening to me? I just went through a war and now this? Somebody give me a break. What have I done? What is that sound?"

Fear turned to frustration and then to anger. I threw the Bible on the floor, and it landed with an anticlimactic *plunk*. I turned off all the lights, railing in anger at God: "Jesus, if I die tonight, it's all your fault. I don't know what to do. But whatever happens now, it's all your fault."

My second prayer to Jesus, short and sweet. I pulled the sheets off and crawled under the bed, curled up in a fetal position, and, trembling, did my best to reassure myself. *Whatever happens, don't open your eyes. You're good. Nothing can pin you down under here.*

Then, just minutes later, it felt as if someone was shaking

me by my shoulders. *Here we go again*, I thought. *Whatever happens, don't open your eyes.*

I'm not sure how I got there, but I found myself sitting on my bed, eyes wide open. And that's when I saw him. I cannot describe what I saw except to say I was overwhelmed by his presence. Just as I understood the demon's murderous intent as it approached me, I understood with astonishing clarity what Jesus communicated right there, right then:

I am Jesus. Your life is not your own.

For the first time in my life I felt like I belonged. I was at home, and I knew it had nothing to do with geography or nationality. It wasn't religious. This peace was so much more than the peace I had anticipated when I prayed with Mahmood. This was an aggressive, powerful peace. It filled the room. It grew roots in my heart and in my soul. It intoxicated me. *Jesus* intoxicated me. I couldn't keep my eyes open, and yet I couldn't keep them off of him. I was looking at him, and yet I felt like I was inside him. The only thing I knew to say was a teenager's exclamation of joy and wonder: "Cool."

And I fell asleep.

TWO

Mahmood

The family—that dear octopus from whose tentacles we never quite escape, nor, in our inmost hearts, ever quite wish to.

—Dodie Smith

I GUESS YOU COULD SAY it was all Mahmood's fault.

If he hadn't committed the ultimate act of treason—becoming a Christian—I wouldn't have prayed that audacious prayer that stirred hell against me and brought heaven to my rescue. My sister, Obea, would not have heard the gospel from me. The same goes for my other sister, Atiya, and my younger brother, Ali. I would have never met my wife, Ashley. Our two children would not exist. I cannot imagine the fate of our entire family had my oldest brother not had faith in Jesus and been bold enough to tell me about it.

The funny thing is, Mahmood was probably the best Muslim of the lot of us. He is the firstborn. From day one he felt the unshakable responsibility firstborn sons feel in our culture. I wouldn't know firsthand, but I'm guessing it's a lot of pressure. As soon as he turned twelve, my mom was on him to become a better Muslim. He entered Qu'ran reciting contests. These consisted of a teacher or Imam reciting the first lines of a passage and stopping midverse so that Mahmood or the other contestants could finish the passage from memory. Mahmood distinguished himself by coming in second—out of three. He would have won these competitions if he'd been able to recite the verses "cool" enough. The Qu'ran is typically read in a singsong voice, and Mahmood never quite got the hang of it, probably because he never wanted to do it.

He also began to pray five times a day on most days, not just during Ramadan. I have a hilarious memory of the Imam pushing Mahmood's rear end down farther on his prayer rug at the mosque because he wasn't flexible enough to bow properly. I'm pretty sure Mahmood would never be able to do yoga. But being a good Muslim boy was not all that bad. Both Mahmood and I still reminisce about sleeping late and watching TV all day during Ramadan, then chowing down on our mom's great cooking at sunset. The entire country's timetable shifted during those days, and we loved it. Playing outside late at night after feasting with friends and family—what's not to love about that?

Mahmood was serious about Islam. More than I was, at least. He understood that certain things were required of him if he was going to be in right standing with Allah. The sacrifices and the rituals meant something to him. So, if you think about it, the fact that he left home and landed among Christian friends from Kuwait in a Christian college in the United States, well, it's remarkable.

My dad had planted the idea in Mahmood's mind that one day he'd go to the States, but he didn't know how it would happen. Then when Mahmood was a teenager, some friends of his who had moved there the year before—guys he had no idea were Christians—suggested he might like to attend the college they went to in South Carolina. He sent them all his necessary information, and they filled out his application and walked it into the admissions office of Spartanburg Methodist College, where he started the degree he would eventually finish in Charleston. None of us paid any attention to the word *Methodist*. Even if we had, we would never have guessed it had anything to do with Christianity. Within three weeks of applying, Mahmood was on a plane bound for Spartanburg, South Carolina. And not one of us, including Mahmood himself, saw what was on the horizon.

"What's a Hayride?"

Right off the bat, Mahmood's friends told him about Jesus. He was never as hotheaded as I was, so he listened politely. They were his friends, after all, and he trusted them. Not long after he'd arrived in the States, these same friends invited him to a hayride at their church. He had visited the church and knew some of the people there, so he said he'd go. As you can imagine, Mahmood had no clue what a hayride was.

As Mahmood tells it, it was a surreal experience, bumping along in a wagon bed that was covered with a thin layer of itchy hay. Several Cambodian refugees went along, too, looking just as bewildered as Mahmood was. Then they stopped, hopped off the wagon, and gathered in a field for hot chocolate. A man named Phillip, whom Mahmood had met and liked, got everyone's attention. He pulled a fat wallet from his back pocket and held it high in the air so everyone could see it.

"This wallet represents your life—a life that is filled with sin."

Mahmood had no problem making the connection with his own life and that wallet full of sin. What good Muslim wasn't aware that he or she sinned regularly and often? But what Phillip said next sounded inconceivable to my brother.

"Jesus Christ knows all about your sin—past, present, and future. He died to take that sin away—all of it—for all time," he declared as he put his wallet back into his pocket.

Mahmood was incredulous. Could what Phillip said really be true? Did God know about the sin he would commit tomorrow? And did Jesus really make a sacrifice that was big enough, perfect enough, to atone for all his sin? The thought burrowed into his mind like a dormant seed, gathering nutrients for the day it would finally sprout and grow. He couldn't shake it. He thought about it all the time.

Mahmood would tell you that his salvation experience, unlike mine, was a process. He would say it started that night, but it didn't mature and grow until months later. But that doesn't make what happened in his heart any less extraordinary than what happened to me just a few years later. That's because grace itself is supernatural. It is as astonishing as any unearthly experience we might have, as miraculous as the appearance of demons or angels in a dark bedroom. Mahmood was overtaken by grace.

During this time of intense questioning, Mahmood had

a dream. Jesus appeared to him, clear as day, and said, "I am the Way, the Truth, and the Life." Because he had been thinking about Jesus and this very claim so often, he didn't give the dream much thought until later.

Mahmood began to gather and collate (he thinks like that—way more organized than me) all the information he'd heard about this new and dangerous faith. He prayed, *Jesus, if this is real, would you show me?*

He worried about what would happen to his brothers and sisters if he plunged into Christianity. He knew he wouldn't be physically harmed by us or excommunicated, but he wasn't so sure people outside our family would be as accepting. He even wondered if Islam would take him back if he converted to Christianity then changed his mind and wanted back into the Muslim faith. He had grown up in a religious culture that taught him, in no uncertain terms, that if he left it, there would be consequences. He chewed on all of this, all the while surrounded by friends who lived out the gospel and tried to answer his questions as best they could.

Months later, Mahmood went to another event held by the same church. This time a group of bodybuilders gave a demonstration and talked about God, about the devil, and about life. He couldn't help but be impressed when these guys tore phone books in half, bent jail-cell bars, and bench pressed three times Mahmood's weight. But his heart was primed and ready for the main event: the gospel. When the leader said, "Do you think we're cool because we're big? The only thing cool about us is Jesus," Mahmood wondered if maybe there was some truth to this claim.

Toward the end of the presentation, the bodybuilders

preached the gospel clearly and simply. For once, Mahmood didn't think about it. He'd already done that in great detail, and he realized it was time to take the ultimate risk. The body-builders held an altar call, and Mahmood went forward. He had all the information he needed, and he realized he truly believed it. It was decision time. Mahmood asked to be baptized at the next church service, Easter Sunday.

Yeah, it was all Mahmood's fault. And our family is forever indebted to him.

Beyond the Burning Bush

By the time he transferred to the College of Charleston, Mahmood had matured in his walk with Jesus. When I swaggered into his life with my disrespectful questions and taunts, he could handle it. When I pointed to that bush one night as we walked the streets and acted like I expected God to zap it and make it burn, Mahmood was patient with me. He was equipped to share his faith not just with me but also with others. After I joined him in following Jesus, we both continued to learn more and more about telling others about Jesus, especially our Muslim friends.

What I learned from Mahmood during that time has proven invaluable to this day in my ministry. He taught me that there are three components to effective evangelism.

1. The Knowledge Component

It would be easy for me to walk away from Islam and never look back, but looking back is precisely what I must do if I am going to engage Muslims with the gospel. I need to remember my heritage, and I need to be conversant with the belief system my culture is founded upon. This knowledge enables me to have intelligent conversations and to keep the dialogue going toward truth. It also enables me to avoid offending my Muslim friends unnecessarily. For example, if I understand the history of Islam, I'll know to stay away from glowing remarks about the Crusades. If I understand Islamic laws and culture, I'll know many Muslims consider representational art—including religious art—to be tantamount to idolatry. I'd think twice about using a tract with a picture of Jesus on it because most Muslims would consider this an icon of my faith, a sign that I worship an idol, not God himself. The more I know, the more sensitive and caring I can be, and the more I can relate the gospel in terms my Muslim friends can understand. We have to care about people before we try to convince them.

2. The Emotional Component

Simply because he has dark skin and looks Middle Eastern, Mahmood has been approached by random strangers in the mall or the grocery store who invite him to church. Not cool. No one wants to be singled out based on his or her racial, ethnic, or religious profile. Muslims are no different. Because so many mission agencies and ministries target Muslims these days, it is especially important to build a relationship and a tight emotional bond with Muslim friends before sharing the truth of the gospel with them. Again, no one wants to sense that they are in the crosshairs of every Bible-toting Christian out there. Of course, building a relationship isn't always possible, and there are times when sharing with someone "cold" is exactly the right thing to do, but in most cases the gospel travels most effectively along relational lines.

3. The Spiritual Component

Not long ago a man brought his Muslim wife to me and asked me to share the gospel with her. I could tell from the get-go that she had been pressured into coming to see me and wasn't in the least bit interested in hearing what I had to say. I shared my story and the message of Jesus with her. I could see she had a lot of questions, but her shyness was getting the better of her. So I suggested, "Why don't you seek God earnestly and ask Jesus to reveal himself to you? If you do that—daily and sincerely—for one month and nothing happens, you can stop."

I could tell her husband was furious with this plan of action. He looked at me like, *That's it?*

But let's think about it. Salvation is, in the final analysis, always accomplished by supernatural means, not human means. No one can understand the gospel, much less accept it, without the work of the Holy Spirit. In the end, we must always relinquish the person and his or her decision to Jesus. He said, "No one can come to me unless the Father who sent me draws him" (John 6:44). Bottom line: God is in control of this stuff; we're not.

If the guy who brought his wife to see me had stuck around long enough, I would have told him not to fret if he didn't see God at work right away. (I'd have told her that, too, but he got her out of there so fast, I didn't have the chance.) I would have opened the Scriptures and pointed to Jeremiah 29:13: "You will seek me and find me, when you seek me with all your heart." Clearly God desires to be found, and he can be trusted to reveal himself at the right time. Our only task is to seek him; his love for us does the rest.

If we are going to engage Muslims in ongoing gospel conversations, all three of these components—intellectual, emotional, spiritual—must be present to some degree. I thank Mahmood for giving me this balanced perspective early on. He did not doubt the supernatural, downright weird way I came to Christ, but he knew I needed to become mature enough to ground the telling of my story in truth.

RISKY BUSINESS

I sometimes ask people this question: Was there a time when you trusted God more than you do now?

It's one of those personal questions I feel I have the right to ask others because I continually turn it on myself. And I don't always like my answer. I look at Mahmood's story and the domino-toppling effect it had—an effect that goes beyond our family—and I am in awe of God's love, his unmerited selection of us, and his dramatic and deep re-rooting of our family tree, and it's easy to say that I trust God implicitly. But it's even easier to forget our beginnings and, thus, to forget to trust the God of those beginnings.

Not long ago Mahmood reminded me of a time right after I met Jesus when Mahmood and I were on a bus together, and I turned and spoke to the driver as we were getting off. I simply asked him if he knew that Jesus loved him.

Mahmood says that was a bit of a proud moment for him. I was his brother as well as his son in the faith, so he felt a certain gratification in my boldness. But he felt sorrow too. By that time he had already become so indoctrinated into American civility that it sometimes kept him from boldly sharing his faith. As Dumas Malone says, "the boldness of his mind was sheathed in a scabbard of politeness."[1] I can relate to that now. It's easy to trust God less as life goes on and is just plain ordinary for long stretches at a time. As Andy Stanley says, "Past boldness is no assurance of future boldness. Boldness demands continual reliance on God's spirit."[2]

But when I remember our stories, both Mahmood's and mine, I am reminded of God's power. When I repeat our stories, I'm reminded of God's faithfulness and what a privilege it is to know him. When I recount the way he chose me, I am challenged to return to my first love and the courageous way I used to tell others about Jesus.

THREE

STRANGER IN A STRANGE LAND

So you are no longer strangers and outsiders. You are citizens together with God's people. You are members of God's family.

—EPHESIANS 2:19, NIRV

NOT FITTING IN IS SOMETHING I've understood my entire life. It never registered with me, though. It was just who I was, like a badge I wore or a club I belonged to.

I was born in Kuwait to Pakistani parents. Kuwait is a place where you can own absolutely nothing—including citizenship—unless your parents are Kuwaiti. Sixty percent of Kuwait's residents are foreign nationals, which means a big majority of the population is like our family was, renters who depended on the largesse of their sponsors and could be asked to leave at any time. Although my family was Sunni Muslim, my first years were spent in a Catholic school. After that, until fifth grade, I studied in an Indian Hindu school. Not only did my fellow classmates speak a different language and follow a different religion, Indians are typically shorter in stature than Pakistanis, so I towered over my peers. All this, in some subtle way that none of us understood, rubbed salt in the wounds that existed between our two cultures, wounds that had only recently begun to heal. Then I went to a Pakistani school where you'd think my square edges would soften to fit into a round hole. The only problem was I'd never learned to read and write my first language, Urdu. Now, *that* was a problem, since all the course work was in Urdu. Yeah, I majored in not belonging.

Again, I wasn't bothered by any of this. For the most part I enjoyed growing up in Kuwait, living in close proximity to our friends from India who shared our villa. My mom and dad were from big families, but because we didn't live in Pakistan, we didn't see them often. Our fellow expatriate neighbors were our family. I was fine with that, because lots of the kids in our neighborhood were boys my age.

The reason we were in Kuwait was simple. Pakistan is, to use a Cold War term, a third-world country, with all the limitations you'd expect in such an environment. And Kuwait is first world. In Kuwait my parents discovered a better economy, better jobs, better living conditions, and a better education for us. On paper it looked like a good idea, but the decision to leave Pakistan had its negatives. It definitely established my mom and dad as the black sheep of our family, the defectors who thought they were too good for Pakistan.

I had an aunt and uncle who also lived in Kuwait, and during my younger years we were close to their family. There was talk of Mahmood and me marrying their two oldest daughters. It was one of those back-burner discussions; understood but not settled. Then my mother decided to send us to an Indian school, even though that decision made us seem more like snobs than ever to our Pakistani family, including my aunt and uncle in Kuwait. After that, our relationship with them cooled somewhat. This wasn't a problem at the time, but it came back to haunt us many years later.

"No More School"

"No more books. No more teachers' dirty looks." If I had known that ditty as a kid, I would have sung it loud and clear. School was definitely not my thing. And I sure got my share of dirty looks. I don't want to make excuses for myself, but I do want to remind you that I was a Pakistani in an Indian school. There were some significant differences between my classmates and me. They spoke Hindi; I spoke Urdu. Our countries were rivals at best, enemies at worst. They were polytheistic; my family was monotheistic. These things didn't matter much to a second grader, but they provided a somewhat dark backstory to my years in the Indian school. Essentially, it was a setup for failure. I did not fit in. I had friends and I had fun, but I didn't excel academically at all.

Our school looked like a big, brick prison—no joke. Every morning we gathered, whatever our nationality, to sing the Indian National Anthem. All of us were boys. The girls went to school in the morning and the boys in the afternoon. There were thirty to forty in a classroom with one teacher per subject who came to us in rotation, and whose word was law. Or else.

The "or elses" included bloody knuckles from a wooden ruler and chili pepper administered to our young, blinking eyes. And then there were the traditional saris our middle-aged teachers wore that revealed their midsections—rolls of fat and all. Nothing could shut down a young boy's hormones faster.

As I said, I was not a great student. Languages were my fatal flaw, so my Urdu-speaking self was sunk in a school where the spoken language was Hindi and the curriculum was in English. And did I mention that every student had to learn Arabic? Besides, school was just plain hard by any standard. Testing was serious business. In fact, the first time I saw a multiple-choice test was in college in the United States.

My saving grace was my spacious double desk, a little island of private property that no teacher or administrator ever checked. Not that private property was an inalienable right or anything like that; they just never looked there. It was the perfect hiding place for cheat sheets. One night my father stopped in the doorway of the room I shared with my brothers and asked me what I was doing.

"Making a cheat sheet," I responded openly. I guess I just thought it was a viable option, given my circumstances.

"*Naeem, hum ai say nahi karthe* (Naeem, you shouldn't do that)," he said, "*Is ko phank do!* (Throw it away!)."

I made another one in the morning, and passed the test. When cheat sheets weren't viable, I resorted to other tactics. I conned teachers. I sweet-talked classmates.

I had a hard time learning Hindi. When it was my turn to read aloud, I excused myself to go to the bathroom so often that when it was my turn, the teacher would say, "Naeem, don't you need to go now?" Other times, I memorized the section of the book that I would be called upon to read aloud just minutes before my turn would come up. I'm really good at memorizing now, and I attribute that skill to the cheating ways of my youth. I was in survival mode.

Let's put my predicament in perspective. I had to study English, Urdu, Hindi, and Arabic all at the same time. I don't want to excuse bad behavior, but I was just trying to make it out alive. And I pulled it off.

Until fifth grade. Suddenly, the concepts we were learning floated above my head just out of reach, and I couldn't cheat my way into understanding them. I failed fifth grade miserably, and I had to repeat it. Only, in the Indian schools of Kuwait, we don't use the word *repeat*. We insist on calling it *failure*. I failed. So, as a bona fide failure, I tried again. And failed again. Two years of fifth grade ended in utter defeat.

What was life like during these two years as I was sinking deeper and deeper into academic ruin? Not so bad most of the time. There were five kids in our family, and my dad traveled a lot for his work, so I flew under my parents' radar. They understood the Indian school was difficult, so other than a little yelling, they weren't too hard on me. I fell through the cracks; at the time, that was fine by me. Even today the smell of jasmine takes me back to those years and happy memories. More than a little oblivious, I managed to do my own thing most of the time.

At the Indian school, the predominant organized sport was cricket, and I hated cricket. I loved soccer though, and I played it every chance I got. It wasn't organized, and maybe that suited me better. I was a tough kid. I wasn't necessarily a bully, but I did get into fights and I was—especially the second time around—bigger than my Indian peers in fifth grade. I was wild and a little bit crazy, but I adhered to an honor code of my own making. According to my irrational code, if I was going to be bad, it ought to be for a decent reason. Today I can't remember any good reasons for any of the bad things I did.

The second time I failed, my parents weren't as patient. I could tell how disappointed my mother was. My father had had it with me. My sister remembers this as a time when my dad came close to throwing me out of the house. Most of the time I was a typical young boy and blissfully unaware of how bad this situation was. The Indian school wouldn't take me back, so the next year I went to the Pakistani school, where I thought things would get better for sure. Everyone knew Pakistani schools were academically easier than Indian schools. But it was a trade-off. Because they were Muslim schools, they were much stricter about behavior. And of course I had never learned to read and write in my birth language, Urdu—the primary language of my new school—so once again, I wasn't prepared. I took the placement test for sixth grade in the new school and failed it.

The first day of my third go-round in fifth grade, I didn't go. I lied and told my parents the bus didn't show up. That worked for one day. When I finally graced the school with my presence, the teacher met me at the door with a shocked, "You can't be in the right room!" I'd had a pretty big growth spurt over the summer. I was a head taller and two years older than anyone in the classroom. I was even taller than the teacher. She and I argued for a few minutes. She told me there must be some mistake, and I told her I was exactly where I belonged. She picked up a sixth-grade book and handed it to me.

"Can you do this work?" she challenged me.

I wasn't so sure, but I nodded.

"Come with me," she said, pulling me into the hall as if I'd contaminated her room. In reality, she was very kind, just fiercely determined that I was not going to spend one more year as a fifth grader. "Follow me," she said. "Let's go see the principal."

While I waited in the anteroom of his office, she pled my case for thirty minutes before the principal of the school. At least that's what I hoped she was doing behind the closed door. When she emerged, she said, "You have one week to prepare for the sixth grade placement test. The principal wants to see you now." And then she added, "You can do this."

The principal had other ideas. I'll never forget what he said to me in English. He gestured toward the teacher with his eyes locked on me: "She has convinced me you can pass this test. I'm not so sure about that. I know your type. You're a failure, and you'll always be a failure. I expect I'll see you right back in here soon."

FAILING FORWARD

Burn. Sometimes anger is the most productive emotion of all. Something in me snapped that day, and, for the first time, I took responsibility for my academic future. I studied like crazy. My sister had suggested that she could tutor me until I caught up, and I took her up on the offer. I still wonder if the teacher pulled something a little shady to make sure I passed that test, but I passed it, and I went to sixth grade. I got a tutor to help me with Urdu. Because of my years in the Indian school, my

English was better than most of the other kids'. I think my fun-loving personality helped me once the teachers realized I was actually making an effort.

Pakistani schools have awards ceremonies at the end of the year just like schools in the United States. One major difference is that they recognize both the kids who excel *and* the kids who fail. They announce everything, the good and the bad. At the end of sixth grade, I won an academic achievement award. When I crossed the stage and shook the principal's hand, nothing registered on his stern face, no acknowledgment of our first encounter. But I knew I had turned a corner.

It is by the sheer grace of God that most people make it through the middle school years not just alive but with a measure of self worth. And I was no exception. Those first years were rough, no doubt, but after that pivotal sixth-grade year, I came into my own. Sure, there were a few uncomfortable memories, but what kid doesn't have those? There were the shared memories of a Middle Eastern childhood, like the sand in our eyes and mouths during the frequent sandstorms. None of us could forget the ointment our teachers and parents made us put on our eyes in anticipation of those storms, greasy stuff that was almost as annoying as the sand it was meant to repel.

There were the memories I chalk up to my own bad decisions, like the day I punched a Kuwaiti kid. I had a little posse, and my friends and I got into our share of fights. This time what might have been a minor neighborhood-gang fight turned into a stoning of more biblical proportions. The kid's family came after me with rocks and knives. Somehow, I made it out of that one relatively unscathed. What boy doesn't have a legendary fight or two in his adolescent past? I sure had my share of those. I must have been compensating for my insecurities.

I continued to do well academically, or well enough. I was part of a school division called the Iqbal house, and every day I wore my tie with a yellow slash across it that identified me as a member. (Think Hogwarts's Gryffindor or Hufflepuff houses in the Harry Potter books.) I was chosen to represent my house in the quiz competitions. At first I didn't want to do it, but I had a crush on a girl and decided this would be a good way to impress her. My first crush. I competed on a team made up of other kids from my house, and although we didn't win, we didn't embarrass ourselves either.

My memory of these years is a mixture as fragrant as the jasmine plants that grew everywhere in Kuwait and the fresh *roti*s, and their crispier, thinner cousin, *chapatis*, my mother made every day. Every culture has its own version of the bread of life, and *roti* is ours. And then there's *shawarma*, the fast-food staple I grew up on. Chicken, goat, lamb, turkey, or beef grilled to perfection on a vertical spit and served with tabbouleh, fattoush, taboon bread, tomato, and cucumber. Topped with tahini and hummus, there's nothing better. At the risk of alienating readers, I have to admit that I don't like the famous Southern food of the United States. I've acclimated to my new home in many ways, but I refuse to embrace biscuits and fried chicken. And don't even talk about grits. Not when I can still taste and smell *roti*s straight from the cast-iron pan and the savory *shawarma* of my homeland.

During Ramadan we ate only one meal a day, at sunset, but it lasted for hours. We broke our fast with a special drink my mom always made by mixing Pepsi with milk. It sounds gross now, but it was heavenly after a full day of fasting. Then we'd pig out on a meal my mom would go all out preparing. Mahmood and I would stay up till dawn so we could accomplish our goal of sleeping in until dinner at sunset. Most days we woke up around two in the afternoon and had to wait, our stomachs growling, until it was permissible to break the fast. Some of my best memories are of taking off on our bikes at sunrise to explore the neighborhood. Shops didn't open until noon; then they closed at five and reopened late at night.

During these coming-of-age years I had my first girlfriend, Huda, an older girl I'd met during the less-segregated parts of the school day like recess, assemblies, or waiting for the bus. We joined the other kids passing notes to each other in the secret wall where messages scribbled on bits of paper went back and forth between the sexes almost daily. Our culture was like that: the old ways (arranged marriages) mingled with the new (girlfriends and boyfriends passing notes).

Amiji and *Abbuji* (Mom and Dad)

To say my parents grew up in a different time and place is an understatement. My wife, Ashley, and my mom were drinking tea in our living room not long ago, and Ashley decided it was time to fill in some of the gaps in her understanding of my family's history.

"*Amiji* ["mother" in Urdu], when did your mother die?"

My mother stared into her mug for a moment, and said, "When I had my first period, then she died."

A few days before, Ashley had helped Mom fill out a job

application and asked her how old she was. My mother mumbled something about needing to check her passport to find out. These milestones—birth, death, and marriage—are the threadbare facts in the fabric of my mom's history. She was born around the same time Pakistan gained its independence from British India. Her family lost loved ones in the war the history books call the Kashmir dispute. Her mother went to the hospital for surgery when my mom was thirteen, its reason now forgotten, and never came home. My grandfather was a mechanic who worked hard to provide for his family. He never remarried, so my mother relied on her grandmother to teach her the basics of cooking and cleaning for a household. She was not allowed to go to school because an education wasn't considered necessary for girls in those days. Still, she had a desire to learn and begged an uncle to teach her to read and write. Even now, she longs to know English better so she can read to her grandchildren. She knows she was eighteen when she married my father only because that's what she reads on her marriage license.

"What did you do when you lived with your husband's family?" Ashley asked her.

"I took care of their house," she said without any rancor toward the family she'd been thrust upon when she was still a young girl and a new bride, "and I played. I especially loved to jump rope. Until I got pregnant. Then my auntie told me I had to stop."

That's how it was in Pakistan in those days. Girls became women overnight. And men grew up even faster. When my father was sixteen years old, he left Pakistan for Kuwait. He managed to get from his hometown of Lahore to the port city of Karachi, more than seven hundred miles away. He lied about his age, forged papers, and jumped aboard a ship that was headed out into the Arabian Sea, up the Gulf of Oman, and then through the Persian Gulf to Kuwait.

My mom, his cousin, had been promised to him since they were both toddlers, so my dad knew he would have to come back to claim his bride someday. There was no questioning these things in those days. He came home to marry my mom a few years later, stayed in Lahore one full week, and went back to Kuwait. Nine months later, Mahmood was born. My father did not return to Pakistan for two years.

There is some speculation that my dad might never have returned had my mother not urged him to. He was making a life in Kuwait, a good life. His young wife was, he assumed like many a young husband, thriving with his family back home. He'd get around to visiting from time to time. But he eventually came back and took her to Kuwait, where the rest of us were born.

Now that I understand that God is both sovereign and kind, that his control of all things is based on a foundation of intimate love for us and not on a whimsical, far-off disinterest, I can see his plan for my family and me even before I knew him. From Pakistan to Kuwait, and then from Kuwait to South Carolina, of all places, he pursued my brother, then me, then my siblings, until he got our attention in some pretty miraculous ways. We turned and saw that he was chasing us, and by faith we each made the decision to follow him.

But I didn't know any of this back then. All I knew was that by the time I finished sixth grade, I had begun to fit in. I finally felt as if I belonged. At the very least, I felt comfortable enough—because I wasn't merely surviving anymore—to think my own thoughts. No telling where those thoughts would lead one day. When two of my brother's Indian friends convinced him to come join them at Spartanburg Methodist College, a two-year school in South Carolina, the idea began to ferment in my head that maybe someday I'd go to America too.

But first there was an invasion.

FOUR

LIFE INTERRUPTED

Every Iraqi child, woman, and old man knows how
to take revenge . . . They will avenge the pure blood
that has been shed no matter how long it takes.

—SADDAM HUSSEIN

A WAR TELLS A THOUSAND stories, from the tragic to the
heroic. While my experience with war is neither tragic nor
heroic, Royal Air Force Flight Lieutenant John Nichol's is both.
On January 17, 1991, his combat aircraft was shot down in the
first low-level daylight raid of Operation Desert Storm,[1] and he
was forced to eject. That means he exited his plane, accelerat-
ing up to two hundred miles per hour in just under a second at
eighteen times the force of gravity. Nichol says it was like sitting
on "a large rocket-propelled grenade."[2] He was then captured,
tortured, and paraded on television by the Iraqis. Lieutenant
Nichol, who later became a writer, broadcast journalist, and
military commander, eventually credited his experience with
a positive outcome. He said, "It's because of my blackest cloud
that everything I now do has come about."[3]

I was just a teenager during Operation Desert Storm, so my story is nothing like John Nichol's. I was a bystander. But if you superimpose God's sovereign plan on it, everything changes. My story becomes much more than a seven-month interlude that mingled danger with a dose of adventure. It becomes far more dramatic than my life during the war, which included running for cover from a deluge of heavy anti-aircraft shells while waiting in the long line at the bread factory and making sure to avoid the IEDs on our roads. It becomes God's way of making something happen that never would have happened otherwise. It becomes an ejection seat that propelled me closer to the gospel.

Waking Up to War

I was sixteen years old, on summer break and sleeping in on a Thursday, when my mom woke me up to tell me Iraq had invaded Kuwait. It happened in the early morning hours of August 2, 1990, and by the time Mom shook me to wake me up around noon, I wondered how I hadn't heard the Apache helicopters thrumming overhead. I looked outside and counted fourteen of them, low and menacing. It must be true; teenage boys can sleep through anything. Once awake, I saw the dark smoke and heard the explosions in the distance. It wasn't hard to take Mom's word for it. We were officially at war.

While I was sleeping, a hundred thousand Iraqi soldiers, backed by seven hundred tanks, had crossed our borders. Saddam Hussein threatened to turn Kuwait City "into a 'graveyard'" if any other country objected to his "take-over by force."[4] The UN immediately voted to declare Saddam's military actions null and void. But that didn't stop Iraqi special forces from taking over the palace of the Emir, who was also known as the sheikh, the head of the ruling family of Kuwait, and it sure didn't stop the heavy gunfire that killed, some say, up to two hundred people on that day.[5] You may remember Operation Desert Storm as a quick, nearly effortless display of American hubris. The conflict only lasted seven months in Kuwait, with two months of US military involvement, but I remember it as an upheaval of my entire world.

That first day, my dad and I went to the grocery store. It was mobbed, just like grocery stores in the South whenever we see a flake or two of snow. No one knew what to expect, so we all became certified hoarders and bought out the store. We could hear bombs exploding in the distance and tanks rolling by just outside the door of the store. Iraqi soldiers stood around looking intimidating in their desert-colored camouflage and red berets, shouldering their outdated machine guns. Of course, at that time I didn't know that compared to the weapons carried by the Allied forces, these guns were antiques. They could still shoot, so that didn't matter. Later, as foreign nationals fled and Kuwaitis were either captured or nestled underground in hiding, large, open-air markets called *souks* popped up in the city, where vendors sold whatever goods they could find. The Iraqis eventually took over the bread factory, and it became our daily ritual to stand in the long line—right next to the ground-to-air guns—to get bread. The line would disperse whenever the shadows of Allied planes loomed on the horizon. We quickly learned that heavy shells, when shot straight up from the ground, had nowhere to go but down in the aftermath. A falling shell could kill you.

Sometimes this mass panic worked in my favor, and I'd end up with a closer spot in the line after everyone had scattered and all the shells had dropped around us.

We called Mahmood, who had been in the United States just over a year. He told us he had wrecked his car when he heard the news on the radio that day. And then all communication was cut off. We didn't talk to Mahmood again until the end of the war. After that first week, we listened to BBC radio, our only source for outside news.

Just three days later, my dad had a really harebrained idea, so of course I was in on it too. We decided to drive into the city, where most of the action was, to make sure his offices hadn't been destroyed. This was a very real possibility. The streets were completely deserted because nobody in his or her right mind would go there. A few weeks later, we saw what seemed like every bus in the city, from school buses to Greyhound buses, crammed full of foreign nationals who were fleeing the country. Many of our friends left, and we never heard from them again. We drove on streets that were already littered with the ruins of war and literally stained with blood. There were tanks everywhere and wrecked cars on every block. Whole chunks of asphalt had been blown away. It looked like a scene from an Apocalypse movie. As we made our way closer to the city, I looked ahead on one long stretch of road and saw a tank blocking our way in the distance.

"Dad," I warned, "there's a checkpoint ahead. Turn left. Quick!"

Like our original idea, I had the equally harebrained thought that we could outwit the soldiers by getting into the city on back roads. Dad made a hard left into a subdivision, but not before the soldiers at the checkpoint saw us. We made our way through more empty streets, thinking we were home free, until I saw something ahead that was more chilling than the checkpoint. A sniper stood on the roof of a building directly in front of us with his rifle pointed our way. There was no doubt that we were in the center of his crosshairs.

We stopped, raised our hands in the air, and did as he commanded: we backtracked to the checkpoint. Once there, Iraqi soldiers yanked our doors open and pulled us out of the car. I noticed six other detainees lined up and looking as scared as we were. I've never felt more terrified or more helpless. The soldiers interrogated my father, slapping and pushing him around and asking him why he was going into the city. Meanwhile I became more and more convinced that we were going to die.

And then the soldier's phone rang. He stopped and answered it. I'll never know what that was about, but as soon as the call was over he and the other soldiers hopped in their vehicles—jeeps and tanks—and took off. As they left, they warned the eight of us to stay away from the city, or they'd kill us.

WAR: WHAT IS IT GOOD FOR?

Bottom line: the reason for the war was power, which in the Middle East means oil. No surprise there. Saddam Hussein claimed that Kuwait had been stealing Iraq's oil. There was some truth to this claim. Our oil reserves spread deep underground into Iraqi land. While Saddam was busy fighting Iran and consequently not producing any oil, we were pumping away at our wells, wells that reached far underground into Iraq, and getting rich in the process. Saddam's military pursuits had landed him in a lot of debt, and he hoped his conquest of Kuwait would settle his accounts.

Hussein also accused the royal family of some very un-Muslim-like excesses. There was even more truth in this claim. The sheikh's family members were secret party animals. Well, not all that secret since everyone knew all about their lifestyle. But the sheikh himself, Sheikh Jaber al-Ahmad al-Sabah, was a popular leader, and, compared to his peers in other Middle Eastern countries, he lived somewhat modestly. With a net worth of close to four hundred million dollars, I'm guessing his lifestyle was not all that modest by our definition.[6] No one knows exactly how many wives he had or how many children he fathered. He was known to the Kuwaiti people as *Baba Jaber,* or Father Jaber. Just before the invasion, he fled to Saudi Arabia, and his younger half brother, Sheikh Faud al-Ahmad al-Sabah, stayed behind to guard Dasman Palace, the royal residence. Within an hour of the invasion, at what became known as the Battle of Dasman Palace, he was shot and killed. In a public display of aggression only the likes of Saddam Hussein could devise, soldiers placed his body in front of a tank and ran it over.

The war began with a lot of blustering by the Iraqis, who claimed a right to Kuwait. Even at the end of the war, as his defeated army retreated back over its borders, Saddam said,

> Iraqis will remember and will not forget that on 8 August, 1990, Kuwait became part of Iraq legally, constitutionally and actually. They remember and will not forget that it

remained throughout this period from 8 August 1990 and until last night, when withdrawal began.[7]

It sounded a little like the roar of a toothless lion, but that was Saddam's style.

But the trash talk wasn't limited to the Iraqis. It is commonly known that Saddam had promised Kuwait to Yasser Arafat, then leader of the Palestine Liberation Organization. Many of our Palestinian neighbors began to boast as if Kuwait was now their country. We heard rumors that Palestinians were giving away government secrets to the Iraqis and even informing on their former Kuwaiti employers. But not all Palestinians acted this way. We had close Palestinian friends who helped us buy goods that we couldn't have gotten otherwise at the *souks*. We leaned heavily on these friends during the war, and they graciously shared what they could with us.

I grew up with a form of racism. If a Pakistani were standing in line anywhere, it was a settled fact that any Kuwaiti citizen could go ahead of him or her. Actually, if you were *anybody* but a Kuwaiti, you took a backseat. The caste system in Kuwait went something like this: first, the Kuwaiti nationals, next Palestinian and Jordanian Muslims, then the Egyptian Muslims, then the Pakistani Muslims. After us came the Indians, the Filipinos, and, at the very bottom, all the other non-Muslims. Interestingly, Europeans and Americans were treated with respect. But like everything else, the war disrupted the neat categories we'd all just come to accept.

During the war, the Kuwaiti nationals naturally fared the worst. The Palestinians were suddenly in such favor that many Iraqi soldiers, as things began to deteriorate for Hussein, pretended to be Palestinian soldiers and defected to Kuwait, where they felt they would eventually have a better chance at freedom and safety. An Iraqi soldier jumped into our car one day as we were idling in traffic and begged for our help. He, like most of the Iraqi soldiers, had been forced into military service. He told us the government had shot both of his parents, and he wanted out. There was nothing we could do for him, so he hopped out and tried another car.

One day while we were eating breakfast, Iraqi soldiers pounded on our door and barged into our home, announcing that we now had a new citizenship. They demanded that we fill out paperwork to that effect and told us we had three weeks to renew our driver's licenses. Over time, the Iraqi soldiers began to occupy the homes in our neighborhood because we lived near the beach, and they needed easy access to the Gulf. Our cousins found an abandoned villa that, like ours, was divided into four units, but was closer to the city, and we moved in. Apparently another guy lived there too—a Kuwaiti military official who was hiding from the Iraqi army. I never once saw him.

These were the same cousins Mahmood and I were supposed to marry one day. Mahmood's potential marriage to the first daughter was out of the question by then, as he was far away in the States. But, in a loosely arranged sort of way, I still had dibs on the second daughter. She was a nice girl and pretty, too, but I wasn't interested. As you can imagine, it was uncomfortable living in the same house with her. One morning my foot accidentally brushed hers under the table at breakfast. I thought, *Oh no!* and she, from the look on her face, thought, *Oh yes!* After that it was even more awkward. My parents knew I liked my cousin but wasn't interested in marrying her. Everyone dropped the subject during the chaotic aftermath of the war, and I was off the hook.

FAMILY FEUD

My father wanted to stay behind and send the rest of us back to Pakistan. I've already mentioned that my family did not know how to handle conflict. Well, here we were in the middle of an *international* conflict that had very personal implications. The war demanded we make decisions. And my parents could not agree on any of them.

My father had worked his way up in a successful air-conditioning business. He later bought and developed a wholesale construction-supply company in a partnership with two Kuwaiti businessmen. He traveled extensively throughout China and Europe. Dad was the acting CEO of his company, with offices, retail establishments, and employees to manage. As you can imagine, the widespread looting of our city, the bombings, and the economic instability caused by the war had a negative impact on his business. He had many Indian employees who remained in Kuwait, but he eventually had to sell most of his shops. The truth is, my father never fully recovered from the war. At the outset he simply felt Kuwait was neither stable nor safe for his family. But my mother and I disagreed with him. In Mahmood's absence, my opinion now ranked pretty high (at least I liked to think it did). I could be as stubborn as my father.

The only way anyone could leave the country—which

was now considered part of Iraq—was through Baghdad. From the beginning there were rumors of Iraqi soldiers helping themselves to daughters as families crossed the border. The way Mom and I saw it, anything could happen at the border. Even if getting out had been a danger-free option, none of us would have wanted to go to Pakistan. With the exception of my mother, none of us had spent any time in Pakistan other than one quick visit when I was a young boy. By all accounts it was dirty, impoverished, and backward compared to Kuwait. We didn't agree with many of the cultural traditions there, either, especially the arranged marriages between first cousins that were often forced upon couples whether they wanted them or not. My parents were progressive enough that they believed these arrangements should be optional. Besides, we were the outcasts in the family because we'd abandoned Pakistan years before; we weren't sure what kind of welcome we'd receive there. In our minds, sticking it out in an occupied Kuwait was better than living in a foreign place like Pakistan.

Ours was not a unique conflict. It seemed as if the entire country was divided about this very issue. Within the first week of the war, as if they'd listened to my dad's advice, half of the population of Kuwait fled the country. Four hundred thousand Kuwaiti nationals left, including several thousand diplomats.[8] Close to one hundred fifty thousand Indian nationals were airlifted out by the Indian government.[9] The other half, as if in agreement with my mom and me, stayed. For seven months, our family squared off against one another. Inside our own house, as you may imagine, tensions remained high. What started as a battleground quickly turned into a demilitarization zone where we employed our favorite tactic: the silent treatment punctuated with an occasional outburst. I remember weeks of not speaking to my dad. Ultimately my mom and I won by default, because in the seven months the war lasted we never reached a final verdict.

WHAT IS AND WHAT MIGHT HAVE BEEN

Almost as quickly as it had begun, the war was over. In the face of opposition from the United States and its allies, Saddam could not maintain his hold on Kuwait. When the Iraqi army left, they did as much damage as they could on their way out. They burned oil wells. They blew up empty buildings, my school included. They camped out in schools during the war because those were the buildings best suited to housing an army. They also knew the Allied forces would think twice before bombing a school because they didn't want the bad press. I had been about to start ninth grade when the war started, and now I had missed the entire school year. I was already behind schedule. The first school to open up was the Indian Catholic girls' school my sisters attended. The school worked out a deal so that boys could attend as well, but none of our classes were legitimate. We had no choice but to attend this school, but we didn't get any credit for going. I wasn't any closer to graduation than I had been before the war began.

I was too young to work full time, but I was quickly becoming too old for school. Mahmood had gotten into an American college by virtue of his good grades and his high school diploma, and my sister did the same a few years after me, but I didn't have a diploma and wasn't sure I'd be getting one anytime soon. Even if I graduated, my grades weren't good enough to recommend me to most colleges. I was stuck.

Meanwhile, I'd developed a good reason to stay in Kuwait. I met a girl I'll call Rheena at the Catholic school I attended after the war, and we quickly developed a serious relationship. She was my sister Obea's friend, an Indian Muslim from a family that was progressive enough to allow her to go on actual dates with me. Rheena was my first love. She broke up with me after about six months, offering no reason why. I was devastated. Then, not much later, my family made plans for my move to the States.

The night before my flight she called me, and we talked until early morning, rekindling my interest in her and, I hoped, hers in me. I figured I'd stay in touch with her and most likely marry her someday, but fool around with some American girls for the time being. I know, I know; I was basically a jerk. After I met Christ and my world turned upside down, I didn't know who to tell and who not to tell at first. So I didn't tell Rheena. We stayed in touch for a while, but we communicated less and less until we didn't anymore. End of story. (Or so I thought. Years later, after the advent of social media, we reconnected briefly, and I finally got to talk with her about Jesus.)

This romantic drama aside, my present situation looked pretty bleak, all because of a seven-month war. Had the war never taken place, I would have gotten the girl and the job and the life I thought I wanted. But God does not exist in the what-might-have-beens, in the opportunities missed or the disasters avoided. He exists in the middle of *what is*. Even though God is the God of the present tense, sometimes it's useful to think about what might have been. It's helpful to stop and compare what might have been with what is. These things remind us of the miracle of what is. They remind us that God is the only one who controls all things. We do not dictate when or if disaster will strike. We do not have any control over the politics or the machinery of war. And we do not have the power to end a war or to alter the consequences it creates in its wake.

I wonder if, thousands of years ago, Joseph (son of Jacob) ever thought about what might have been. He sure had plenty of reasons to doubt that the I AM of Abraham, Isaac, and Jacob was in charge. I wonder if he asked God about that while he waited to die in the pit his own brothers threw him in, or when they changed plans and sold him for twenty shekels to a bunch of smelly Ishmaelites, or when Potiphar's wife acted like a desperate cougar and couldn't keep her hands off of him, or when Pharaoh's cupbearer forgot all about him and left him to rot in prison. I wonder.

We have the whole of Scripture and millennia of history to help us interpret what Joseph said about his own long list of tragedies—a list much longer and more traumatic than mine. Because it's so familiar to us, his take on things may not sound as startling as it really was. But it's crazy if you think about it. Think about what it took for Joseph to say this to his brothers, the ones who started the chain reaction of calamities in the first place: "You intended to harm me, but God intended it for good to accomplish what is now being done, the saving of many lives" (Gen. 50:20 NIV). Here's a guy who not only trusted in God's sovereignty with every fiber of his being, he understood God's purpose behind every move he made or didn't make. The events of Joseph's life weren't orchestrated merely to save him. They were meticulously planned by a loving God to use him to save others. Joseph knew that.

In the same way, the Gulf War, in my life, was all about God's sovereignty. He planned all along not only to rescue me from darkness but also to use me to call others out of darkness. The *what is* was huge, just beyond what I could see on my horizon. But I didn't understand any of that back then. All I knew then was what I had lost, a long list of what-might-have-beens.

If the Gulf War had never happened, I would have most likely married Rheena. I might or might not have finished school. I would have entered the business world in Kuwait. This would have been my unavoidable path, all because of my own desires at the time, because of my family's influence, and because of the dictates of my culture. Without a Gulf War, I would have stayed glued to the ejection seat, stuck instead of catapulting, as God intended, into the exact place I needed to be to hear the gospel, to discover his kingdom, and to answer him when I heard his voice.

My father recognized that I was stuck. In fact, he felt a certain responsibility for my situation, so he set a plan in motion to unstick me. This plan involved getting tourist visas for every member of our family. He explained to the foreign minister that his oldest son was in the United States, and we needed to reassure him in person that we were okay, you know, after the war and all. He kept saying "we," but all along my father planned to send me—only me—to the States.

A tourist visa at that time could last up to six months max, so if I stayed in the United States any longer than that, I'd be illegal. We were all keenly aware of this fact. When I went through customs in the Miami airport, I asked for the full six months, but I was allotted only one. Not that it mattered. My father felt so strongly that I should leave Kuwait, he just accepted that a necessary part of his plan would involve my illegal-alien status for at least some of my time in the States. It was inevitable. When I got here, I requested an extension of my visa and was denied. When I became a Christian, I was still legal, but not for long. I'd only been here three weeks, so I had one full week of legal status left.

During this part of my story, I can see a stack of what-might-have-beens as high as the three Kuwait Towers that sit on a promontory of the Persian Gulf. If I had graduated from high school in Kuwait, there's no way I would have been admitted as a student, provisional or otherwise, at the College of Charleston. The grades I had made up until the war stopped my schooling were that bad. But because I had no records, they took their chances with me. Also, if I had not become a Christian when I did, I might have remained illegal and risked deportation. (There was a brief period when I was illegal, but don't tell anyone.) An Indian pastor, Pastor Satish Raiborde (a man you'll hear more about soon), befriended me early on and suggested that I apply for religious asylum. The only other way to get legal status was to get married, and that wasn't looking like an option anytime soon. Now that I was a Christian I couldn't go home to Kuwait. Under Islamic law, I could be punished for my conversion to Christianity. I hadn't thought about that. I applied for asylum and was accepted. This was before 9/11, thankfully, so the process was more lenient, and I got in.

I think I only grasped a hint of what God was doing. Jesus' first words to me were not, "Whew! You're safe now with me." No, he said, "I am Jesus Christ, your Lord. Your life is not your own." Thanks to this initial heads-up from Jesus himself, I knew there was more to our relationship than my own comfort and safety. There was even more to it than belonging. I didn't have a clue what the "more" was, but I knew my purpose was much bigger than me.

FIVE

STRANGER IN A STRANGE LAND, PART TWO

God has no problem with spiritual eccentrics.

—ERWIN MCMANUS

I MET JESUS BEFORE I met the church. It's a good thing, too, because the church confused me. Jesus appeared to me and told me my life was not my own, and I believed him. I knew him like I knew a friend. I started reading the Bible with the Jesus I was still getting to know in my mind, and it just blew me away. I wasn't confused by *him*; no, I was in awe of him.

Church . . . now that was another matter. First there was the "getting saved" thing. I wasn't sure I'd actually done *that*, so every single time a pastor or Bible-study leader led us in a sinner's prayer, I prayed it. I got saved a bunch of times. I got saved at small Bible studies and in big church services, in my living room watching TV preachers and in conversations with well-meaning Christians. I later began to think that there were

57

a lot of people in churches who wanted to be saved but didn't want to meet Jesus.

Christians were just plain weird. A lot of things mattered to them, and I, for the life of me, couldn't figure out why some of those things were so important—like denominations. I was stunned when I discovered how many distinct varieties of churches there were and how much animosity existed between them. In Islam there are four basic groups. Only four. I initially thought Christianity was even less divided than Islam, as in Protestants and Catholics and that's it. But was I wrong.

The church was my new family, so in the best sense of the word I was finally at home. But I still didn't fit in. The Southern Baptist church Mahmood and I and all our FCA friends went to was great, but I did not fit in there—at all. I wasn't the right color. My hair was long back then, pretty shaggy compared to my new, clean-cut Baptist friends. I didn't wear khakis and blue blazers. For a while, I still smoked. No one could relate to my past. I didn't "get saved" the same way they did, so even on that level it was hard to find common ground in my new environment. I was a foreigner in a foreign country with a shaky visa status, which made assimilating a challenge. And I had this crazy story.

I started telling my story to people, and I'd watch them shut down. They had been praying for me, but this was *not* how they expected their prayers to be answered. It didn't fit any paradigm they knew. They responded with subtle disapproval or outright shock, and they made it seem as if this kind of thing "didn't happen," at least not in the United States. I was, according to some veteran Christians, imagining things. My story unsettled them, and their reactions to it made me more than a little paranoid. I'll tell more of my church story later, but for now just know I had a lot to learn. I wish I'd read Dallas Willard back then. He would have believed me. He not only wrote that we *could* hear from God, he implied that we *should*: "People are meant to live in an ongoing conversation with God, speaking and being spoken to."[1]

I wish I'd known my friend Erwin McManus too. He definitely would have believed me. In his book *The Barbarian Way*, he describes how the church might react if John the Baptist showed up on the scene today. Compared to this dude, my story wasn't quite so strange:

> Is it possible that God is the cause of such abnormality? How many of us would actually expect the person who came to prepare the way for the coming of Christ to present himself wearing animal skins, eating locusts, and wandering around in the desert? If he lived today, he would be medicated and diagnosed bipolar. He would be one more certified lunatic. And that's just what would happen if the church were in charge of his diagnosis. Most of us would think John was out of his mind.[2]

The problem was, the crazy stuff kept on happening. Mine was not merely a one-episode story; it was an ongoing one. Either something real was up between God and me, or I was going nuts. There were times when I feared my new church friends might be right, that I was indeed mentally unstable. But, even more terrifying to my soul, I had another fear that went something like this, "What if it happens again and Jesus doesn't show up?" I didn't have long to guess about that one.

Not long after my first encounter with Jesus, Mahmood and I spent Thanksgiving at his girlfriend's parents' home. One afternoon we went to the mall. When we got back, I was tired, so I sat on the pullout sofa in their den and stretched out with my feet still on the floor. Mahmood and his girlfriend were nearby in the living room where I could see them. Suddenly I felt something clamp down on each of my wrists. I looked and there was nothing there. But I couldn't move my arms. I yelled for Mahmood and his girlfriend, but they couldn't hear me. Then I did what came naturally: I trash-talked Satan with every ounce of indignation I could muster.

"You're nothin'! Is this all you got?"

Let's just say it wasn't very effective. During my first episode with demons I could move my head from side to side, but this time I couldn't. I was paralyzed. Then I "saw" a demonic face (I'm using quotations here because I don't think I saw with my physical eyes, but the impression couldn't have been clearer) and felt it claw at my ear. It's as if two worlds—the spiritual and the physical—were on a collision course, and I was in the middle observing them both. It was kind of like an out-of-body experience.

"Stop," said a voice I immediately identified as Jesus. And it all stopped. Now I knew that Jesus was there for me, that he had authority, and that I could trust him to handle anything Satan threw at me. I was so grateful that I began to weep. That's when Mahmood and his girlfriend came in to check on me. They'd heard me making noises, but they thought I was asleep. By then the attack was over. Until the next time.

I continued to have harrowing encounters with demons. I got slapped and pushed around. It often happened right when I was falling asleep. Mahmood began sleeping with me because it was so terrifying. It's kind of pitiful, really. He was right there to observe it all, the panic and the literal thrashing about in a fight with the demonic world.

During this time I met my first "spiritual dad," Pastor Satish. His church was two hours away in Columbia, South Carolina, so I only went there when I could get away. Talk about a far cry from the Baptist church. Pastor Satish introduced Mahmood and me to Raj and Manu, an Indian couple who adopted us into their family and created a home away from home for us. They also allowed me to work for them at a store they owned called High Fashion New York, selling expensive, gangster clothing: alligator shoes, gold chains, and leisure suits.

Mahmood convinced me I should tell Pastor Satish my story, including the details of the most recent attacks. Until then, the people who actually believed me told me I was special. Mine was a one-of-a-kind experience, they said. And I believed them. But that didn't make what was happening any less frightening.

Pastor Satish asked me one simple question: "Are you reading your Bible at night?" I wasn't. He also told me countless stories, many of them his own, that made mine seem rather tame. He was trying to commit suicide the first time Jesus appeared to him. To tell the truth, I wasn't reading my Bible at night because I was more than a little afraid of it and, until I met Pastor Satish, who could blame me? After that I started reading it every night, and the attacks lessened dramatically.

GROWING PAINS

Have you ever wanted to take back a moment when something you said or did was not true to who you are? We remember those kinds of moments with clarity—like the time I ate dinner with Mahmood and an Indian friend of ours who was Hindu at a local college hangout. The three of us had had several discussions about Christianity. During dinner an Arab guy, someone I'd seen around, came up to our table, and said, "Hey, I'm Amir."

I introduced him to Mahmood and our friend, "Amir, this is my brother, Mahmood, and our friend, Paami."

"So, you're Muslim, right?" he asked.

"Yeah," I said.

"What's that cross you're wearing then?"

"This? It's just, you know, fashion."

He left as quickly as he'd come, and I immediately thought, *What did I just do?*

Mahmood looked at me with the same question in his eyes. Even our Hindu friend seemed disturbed by my lack of loyalty to Jesus. Paami grinned at me and said, "So you're Muslim again?"

I was devastated. Wasn't there something like, "If you deny him, he will also deny you," in the Bible? I had no idea why I'd lied. I was shocked into silence for the rest of the night. Afterward, as soon as I was alone, I cried out to Jesus, "What did I just do to you?"

One of the first psalms I read as a new Christian was Psalm 51. From the beginning I related to David. I knew good and well that I was a sinner. I had cheated my way through school. I was a fighter. I wasn't a good son or a good brother. Basically, I wasn't a good guy. No one had to tell me that the things I did and said were bad. I already knew. But this was different. This time I'd hurt Jesus. I had damaged our relationship.

I pinpoint this time as a historic moment in my life, when I finally realized I was forgiven for wounding Jesus, and I felt, for the first time, the full weight of grace. Psalm 51 became my constant prayer:

Create in me a clean heart, O God, and renew a right spirit within me. Cast me not away from your presence, and take not your Holy Spirit from me. Restore to me the joy of your salvation, and uphold me with a willing spirit. (Ps. 51:10–12)

I knew my only hope was for Jesus to create a clean heart in me just as he did in David. And he began to do it, slowly and over time. The next year, when my sister Obea explained to a friend why she finally decided to follow Jesus, she said, "I could argue about Jesus and Muhammad, but I couldn't argue with the way my brother Naeem changed."

A few years later I was much more settled in the fact that I was an ex-Muslim. I worked in a retail store in downtown Charleston, one of many jobs that got me through college. One day an Arab man walked into the store, shopped around a little, and then came to the cash register to pay for his merchandise. He introduced himself to me, probably hoping I was from his part of the world, and said, "Naeem, love that name. You're Pakistani, right?"

"Yeah, I am."

"You're Muslim too?"

I didn't hesitate. "Well," I said, "I was, but I'm not anymore."

I told him an abbreviated version of my story. I watched as, in a split-second, his demeanor toward me changed radically, and he said, "You have done a very bad thing."

He put his purchases down on the counter as emphatically as he could without violently throwing them down and walked out of the store. He was obviously displeased, but there was no doubting that Jesus was pleased with me in that moment. I was learning to love him more than the world.

You'll never find one moment in the gospels when Jesus was ashamed to admit his relationship to his Father. I was glad I was finally mature enough to mirror his courage somewhat, to cast aside the fear of men like he did (Heb. 13:6). But Jesus was more than bold. He didn't boast about who he was. He wasn't afraid to love people. That means that although he valiantly spoke the truth, he grieved when people didn't accept it . . . or him. As I grew, I began to see that faith was about much more than being unafraid. It was about loving people and allowing them to choose whether or not they would love you back.

It doesn't cost us that much to tell a stranger about Jesus. But our friends and our family; now that is a different story. Telling those we love doesn't just stretch the faith muscle; it exercises the heart muscle too. And it can cost us deeply.

ARVIND

Arvind was my older brother's friend in Kuwait. So of course I wanted to be friends with him too. Arvind was way cooler than I was. He drove; I didn't. He was friends with all the party people; I wasn't. His family was rich; mine wasn't. He lived in a villa that was split into two apartments instead of five like ours. (This was one of the undisputed signs of affluence in Kuwait. The fewer units in your building, the better off you were.) He introduced me to his set of friends—most of them Catholic and older than me. I suppose at the time this seemed very exotic to a sixteen-year-old. Not that Arvind was merely a rung on my ladder to coolness. We shared the kinds of memories teenagers share in almost every culture and, in the process, became close friends.

Alcohol is hard to come by in a Muslim country. But we managed somehow. Because of the American and European influences after the war, Kuwait became more liberal and alcohol was easier to buy. But before the war it was one of those elusive taboos none of us could resist. I remember chipping in with Arvind and a bunch of friends to buy a bottle of Johnny Walker Red for one hundred dinars. That's about three hundred bucks. We literally met some dude in an alley and exchanged our money for the bootleg booze. One bottle between a bunch of kids wasn't enough for anyone to get drunk, so the whole thing was pretty anticlimactic. I guess you could say Arvind and I had forged a friendship based on liquor, cigarettes, similar world views, and adventure. Sounds pretty typical for a lot of teenage boys in the States.

In 1996 Arvind came to Charleston for a weeklong stay with us. He had come for a few days in 1993, so he already knew I was different from our Kuwait days, but in that first visit I had not given him any clues as to why I had changed. I looked forward to this visit because we'd had fun the time before, and because this time I wanted to explain to him about Jesus. As soon as he got here, there was a rift between us because I wouldn't smoke, drink, or swear with him. I know it sounds shallow, but that didn't leave much else to connect us. He knew I had changed, but how and how much was an unknown to him.

Mahmood and I invited him to go to an FCA meeting with

us, and he went just to be polite, but he made a not-so-subtle statement by wearing a T-shirt that was emblazoned with a shockingly inappropriate message on the front. He tolerated the meeting, and as soon as it was over, he was itching to get out of there. He said, "Let's go shoot some pool."

I agreed, hoping we could talk. We went to a pizza place that turned into a bar and pool hall after hours. Arvind proceeded to drink. Eventually he got into a fight, and before long the bouncer got involved. That's when I stepped in and almost got knocked out as the three guys went for one another with me in the middle. Never a dull moment with Arvind. Not only did we get thrown out, the owner—an acquaintance of mine—came after us with a billy club. That was a first for me.

I tried to grab Arvind's keys, but he insisted on driving. We argued and I lost, so he left without me, circled the block, and came back to get me. No way was I letting him go alone in a car. By this time my mom, my sisters, and my younger brother had all come to the States and were living with Mahmood and me in a cramped apartment. I dreaded waking up the whole household, but I knew the minute Arvind walked in the door it was inevitable. By the time we both made it home, Arvind had calmed down, but only a little. I decided there was no time like the present to tell him my entire story. I'm not sure there was a better time, but this one didn't go so well. I ended up throwing Bibles at him (I know, really mature of me), and he picked up a bottle of cologne and came at me with it. Something stopped him in his tracks; I'm guessing it was what stopped me too. We were brothers, and we loved each other. Arvind stalked out and sat on the stairs outside our apartment, and I followed with a blanket and sat next to him.

I'd like to say we had a great conversation then and that Arvind finally believed in Jesus, but that's not what happened. He left the next morning, still annoyed with me. I wish Arvind fully understood my relationship with Jesus, but I think he's getting there.

A year after the fateful 1996 visit, Arvind called me from New York when he was there on business. The call was short, but ended with an "I love you, man," from Arvind. Last year I preached a sermon series about other faiths called "Co-Exist," and he surprised me by agreeing to watch it. He surprised me even more by reporting that he'd loved it. He called one day to tell me about a friend who had been in a car accident, and I asked him if I could pray with him on the phone. He later said, "I don't know what happened when you prayed, but *something* happened."

The Domino Effect

The year after I started school in the States, my sister, Obea, applied to the College of Charleston and got in. Seeing her in person was like guzzling a potent antidote for homesickness. The three of us shared a one-bedroom apartment away from campus. Mahmood slept in the living room, while Obea and I shared the bedroom. Her very first day here, I tried to give her some space to rest once we got to the apartment. I knew how exhausting the first day in a new country can be, so I was surprised when late that night as I was drifting off to sleep she said, "Hey, Naeem, are you awake?"

I assured her that I was. "Are you like Mahmood?" she asked.

"Let's talk," I said.

We went to the living room, and I told Obea everything. Just like the time I finally admitted I was an ex-Muslim to an Arab customer in the store, this was a defining moment for me. Once Obea knew, the rest of the family would eventually have to hear as well. I wasn't exactly thrilled at the prospect of the cat getting out of the bag. I was terrified. I waited for a response from her but got nothing. I looked at her, and I could tell she was shocked, but she started to cry. For several days, Obea didn't speak to me. To Mahmood, yes, but not to me, which I didn't think was very fair. He'd started this whole thing, after all.

When I say I didn't think it was fair, I mean it. A few days later, while I was still getting the silent treatment, I went with Obea, Mahmood, and some of our friends to the Isle of Palms. I walked down the beach away from the others. The pounding surf drowned out my words as I said out loud to the wind, "I don't like you, Jesus. I understand what you said about loving you more than my mother or father or brothers or sisters, but I don't like it. I can't believe I've lost Obea. Now it looks like I'm going to lose everyone. But I don't care. I'm in this for life. I love you, and I'll follow you." And then I added a desperate afterthought, "But is there any way I can have my relationship with Obea back?"

We lived together, so eventually Obea had to talk to me. When classes started, she softened even more, but just a little more. I couldn't invite her to church, but our friends could. She went, only to be polite, and things remained chilly between us, but I knew something was happening inside of her. One Saturday night Mahmood, Obea, and I went with some friends to a restaurant in downtown Charleston. The place was packed, and the whole city seemed to vibrate with a party atmosphere. In the middle of all the noise, I felt God say, "Take Obea for a walk. She's going to come to me tonight."

So I turned to her right then and said, "Hey, Obea, wanna go for a walk?"

I'm pretty certain that it's rude in any culture to leave the dinner table in the middle of the meal, especially in public with a group of friends. So I was surprised when she said, "Yeah, let's go," and actually seemed eager to leave with me.

The minute we got out the door, Obea started crying. I was a little bewildered by that, but I could tell God was up to something here. I'm not sure why, but I suggested we turn right and continue our conversation in a nearby alleyway. After a few minutes, I became keenly aware of how strange the whole scenario must have appeared to all the people milling around on the streets. It felt extremely awkward to me. Here we were, a Middle Eastern man and a crying woman who just ducked into an alley. I'm guessing I'd chosen the alley for privacy, but it didn't look right, that's for sure. No telling what people thought.

If Obea felt any of this, she didn't show it. She started talking, but she didn't make any sense. She sobbed in hiccups about me, about herself, about our relationship, and about Jesus. I tried and failed to decipher what she was saying, and I finally said, falling all over myself not to offend her or ruin this moment, "Obea, can I just pray for you? You can repeat after me if you want to, but you don't have to. You can pray along with me in your mind." Mentally, I added, *if you don't have anything better to do.*

I wonder if God was a little impatient with me then, saying, "Naeem, get with it. Let's rock and roll." Obea nodded through her tears, and I started praying. She repeated everything I prayed, so I got serious and poured out my heart to God on her behalf, and then I said, "Amen."

She said, "Amen."

And she hit the ground—fell straight down. She was crying, and I was wondering what just happened. I had no idea what to do. She got up pretty quickly and said something that surprised me.

"I'm free, I'm free," she said over and over.

I had no idea what she was talking about, but I hugged her as I tried to process what just happened. Back inside the restaurant I leaned over to Mahmood and whispered, "She's in."

Toppling the Pillars

"You're not my kids anymore."

That's how my mom greeted the news that I, along with Mahmood, was a Christian. What would she say when I told her about Obea?

In 1995, the remainder of my family came to the United States. Dad's international business dealings earned him the right to come and go as he pleased. The pages of his passport bore so many stamps that it was proof to the United States government that he would not be a drain on the American economy. Compared to the one-month travel visa I had when I first got to the States, his ten-year visa seemed like the ultimate luxury. Unlike Dad, the rest of us had much less secure visa statuses, so we started strategizing right away. We discussed starting a family business so that each of us could get a business visa like Dad's. For the time being, the plan was for him to go back to Kuwait and support the rest of the family from there while we lived here in the States. A month after arriving in the United States he left for Kuwait, little knowing that our business plan would completely evaporate just days after he left.

Mahmood, Obea, and I knew we had to tell our secret to the rest of the family, except for Dad. Telling him was unthinkable. So we waited until he returned to Kuwait to tell Mom. Somehow—I still can't remember how—it fell to me to deliver the news. One Sunday afternoon I asked Mom if she wanted to go for a walk. This time, the story didn't turn out like my walk with Obea. It was terrible—one of the worst days of my life. Mom didn't start screaming at me like I feared she would, but her quiet despair was almost worse. She was in shock. Slowly, almost calmly, words began to pour out of her mouth, a torrent of accusations at herself and, eventually, at me:

"What did I do?

"My only job has been to raise my children right, and this is what happens? I'm a failure!

"I never should have moved to Kuwait. It's all because of the English schools.

"Why did we let any of you come to America? You think America is so wonderful, but it's not. It's not what you think it is.

"You're not my son anymore."

That last one hurt the most. Mom's lament continued as we walked back to the apartment, and then she went into her room and closed the door. I hoped the storm would blow over. But that didn't seem likely. For the next three days Mom stayed in her room, refusing to talk or eat. She was shattered, and we were the reason, which made it impossible to do anything to ease her pain. We couldn't fix it. By Wednesday, she was ready to ask one burning question: "Who is a Christian besides you, Naeem?"

"Mahmood and Obea."

That was not the answer she wanted to hear.

Now may be the best time to give an overview of Islam, to explain how deeply rooted my family was in this ancient religion. You may have heard of the Five Pillars of Islam. These pillars are not theological truths about God or spirituality. They aren't reasons to hope or statements about God's heart toward us. They are the essential duties every Muslim must fulfill if he or she is to be a true Muslim.

SHAHADA

The *Shahada* is a Muslim's confession of faith. It expresses the two fundamental beliefs that make a Muslim a Muslim. The words are important: *LAILAHA ILLALLAH MUHAMMAD RASULULAH* (There is no god but God and Muhammad is the prophet of God). They also recite the *salat*, the daily ritual prayer. Unlike a Christian's confession of faith where the condition of the heart trumps the exact language, the *Shahada* is more like a password required to enter the Muslim community. It must be recited word for word.

SALAT

Ritual prayer is probably the best-known practice of Islam. Five times a day, at dawn (*al-fajr*), midday (*al-zuhr*), afternoon (*al-'asr*), sunset (*al-maghrib*), and evening (*al-'isha*), Muslims face Mecca and bow for prayer, going through a series of different postures. Prayer must always be preceded by ritual washing of the hands, face, and feet called *wudu*. It's important to note that for a Muslim, prayer is not a conversation with God. It is the performance of a ritual, the fulfillment of a binding law. Rather than the natural communication that takes place in a relationship, the *salat* is recitation.

Sawm, or Fasting

I've mentioned Ramadan, but as a holiday that my brothers, sisters, and I enjoyed. I can only imagine that our experience was similar to that of many children, especially the final ten days, *Eid El-Fitr*, when we celebrated the end of the fast. But for the adults, Ramadan meant serious deprivation to honor the giving of the Qu'ran. Many Muslims choose Ramadan as a time to study the Qu'ran at the Mosque, to remind themselves of their commitment to all five of the pillars.

Hajj

Technically, every Muslim is required to make a *hajj*, or a pilgrimage, to Mecca at least once. As far as I can tell, a *hajj* is not a vacation. Once at Mecca, which is in Saudi Arabia, pilgrims circle the *Kaba* (a monument that contains the famous black stone) seven times. There is always a spike in fatalities during the *hajj* because of the number of pilgrims who press around the *Kaba*; invariably, several people are crushed. After the seventh circuit, the pilgrim must either kiss the black stone or, if he or she can't reach it, point to it. For most Muslims, the *hajj* is their Reset button, the chance for a major renovation, which makes sense if you consider that, of all the pillars it may be the most difficult to do. In a performance-based religion, difficulty is highly valued.

Zakat

Giving is central to Islam, but the *zakat,* or alms, is not the same thing as generosity. It is more like a tax, kind of like certain tithes in the Old Testament. This is not to say there are no generous Muslims, but the pillar isn't about generosity. Like all else in Islam, it is about law. About exact adherence to a very strict code of ethics. So much of what Christians experience— being on missions together, pooling resources in order to give more strategically, personal joy in giving—is lost on Muslims because of this law orientation.

These five pillars are the foundation of Islam. They represent what Muslims consider the immutable laws that support all other laws of Islam. I'm not at all opposed to laws, but I now know there are laws that bind us and laws that free us, laws that bring about condemnation and laws that offer grace. In Psalm 119 David wrote, "I run in the path of your commands, for you have set my heart free" (v. 32 NIV). Paul described an even more complete freedom in Romans 8: "For the law of the Spirit of life has set you free in Christ Jesus from the law of sin and death" (v. 2). My prayer for my Muslim friends and family is that they will find this new "law of the Spirit" that can only be found in Jesus, and that they will be set free.

SIX

The Lamb of God

The animal offerings are among the rites decreed by GOD for your own good. You shall mention GOD's name on them while they are standing in line.

—Qu'ran 22:36

One night, just days after Obea had given her life to Jesus, while Mom was still in mourning and not speaking to me, the three of us slipped out of the apartment and went to church. We needed to get away, and we needed our brothers and sisters in Christ to rally behind us. We asked for prayer and were surrounded by the prayers of our spiritual family. I cried so uncontrollably that night that I had to excuse myself from the group. My mother was traumatized by our decisions, and I was traumatized by her reaction to us.

When we returned, Mom was clearly outraged, this time at a new level. She'd been on the phone with my father, and told us that his solution was to ship us all back. It was like the switch between her anger and indignation finally flipped. She started yelling at us, saying the same things she'd said to me nights before, but with the volume all the way up this time. I probably don't need to mention that our family business idea went up in smoke that night. No one ever brought it up again. Amid all the mayhem, I looked over at my youngest sister, Atiya, and I could tell she was bewildered by what was going on.

Atiya had arrived here in the middle of her tenth-grade year. I can't imagine how stressful life was for her, adjusting to American culture, American food, American clothing, and, worst of all, American high school. But at least she had a home and family. That night I could see it on her face: her world was imploding before her eyes. Home wasn't a safe haven anymore; it had become a war zone overnight. I whispered to her to come into my room. I sat on the bed, and she sat on the floor, tears flowing down her face.

What I didn't know then was that Atiya—just weeks before—had prayed a prayer very similar to mine. The fact that we were Christians bothered her. She didn't know what to make of it, other than to be angry that this Jesus had divided her family. "I keep hearing things about you, Jesus," she prayed. "You're the reason my family is falling apart. I need to know if you're real, so if you are will you show me?"

She told no one about this prayer, so when I asked her to follow me into my room, I had no idea God was about to answer *her* prayer, not just mine.

"Atiya," I said as gently as I could, "I know Mom is going crazy right now, but let me explain."

I took a defensive approach and explained that Mom was not upset because of anything I'd done to intentionally hurt her. I hadn't planned any of this. Then I very briefly told her my story. Suddenly I sensed the presence of Jesus in the room. I was getting the hang of this by now, so I simply asked him, "Are you in the room?"

"Yes," he replied, "I am going to touch Atiya right now, and she'll come to me."

Again, I had no clue that because Atiya had been prayed for and anticipated the presence of Jesus, she recognized him right away when he entered the room.

"Atiya," I asked, "do you feel Jesus in the room?"

She didn't hesitate: "Yes."

"Did he touch you?"

Again, "Yes."

"Do you want to know him?" I asked her over the sound of Mom yelling in the background.

She answered that she did, and, right there in that chaotic apartment, Atiya prayed and invited Jesus to take over her life.

"Let's don't tell anyone yet," I warned. "Mom can't handle it."

Then the miracle of what had just happened hit me, and I said, "Atiya, you came into this room a Muslim, and you're leaving a Christian."

She grinned at me and opened the door, letting in the deafening noise of our mother's wrath. Once again I whispered the news to Obea and Mahmood, "There's another one."

PEACE

In my opinion my youngest brother, Ali, had the hardest time of any of us. He moved here at a tough age, just barely into his teens. He fell into the middle of a family drama of epic proportions. He essentially lost his father when my dad decided to return to Kuwait. Not long after Atiya met Christ, my future brother-in-law, Paul, felt led to share the gospel message with Ali. He listened, and then he knew he had to make a decision, as we all do when we encounter the gospel. Ali chose Jesus. Against all odds he made the right decision, and I'm proud of him for that. Then Atiya, who to this day has a special connection with my mother, told her what she dreaded most, that all of her children were now Christians. She reacted just as we all expected. To be honest, she hasn't completely gotten over it yet.

Our family didn't fall apart, though. Eventually my father heard my story, or at least enough of it to understand the choice I'd made. He now knows all our stories. He even asks me sometimes, "How's business?" which is code for "How's it going at that church you pastor?" My mother is proud of me and of our church. They both love Ashley, though when we first started dating we hid our relationship from them. They just assumed Ashley was a friend who hung around a lot, who respectfully wore long sleeves in the sweltering Charleston summer because they were Muslims. That's actually true, but what they didn't know was that Ashley was going to be around for the rest of our lives.

My mom is still Muslim. Dad too.

We've come a long way as a family. Of course I want my parents to encounter Jesus for themselves and to know him as their Lord. But for now I'm grateful for our healed relationship. My parents even lived in our home for three years when our children were small. Because five members of our seven-member family now call Jesus Lord, it makes sense that our family life would be characterized by peace more now than it ever was in Kuwait. He is the Prince of Peace, after all.

My family is a reminder of two things. First, peace is possible between Christians and Muslims. When Christians and Muslims can live together in peace, especially within the same family and even in the same house, the world sits up and takes notice. The stereotypes and the sensational stories tell us this can't be, but we're living proof that it can. Second, the gospel is relevant. Period. The Christians who shared the gospel with me were not well versed in the Qu'ran. I doubt any of them had read it at all. They had not attended seminars on Islam. They could not quote Muhammad to me. They weren't all that culturally sensitive. All they had was the gospel, and that was enough.

The gospel brings about a peace that doesn't make sense in any other context but a relationship with Jesus. Peace with God and peace between people. The indwelling Holy Spirit also brings about a personal, inner peace that enables us to handle any challenge life throws our way. Atiya, for example, needed peace in a way I couldn't imagine at the time. She was a young Muslim girl from a foreign country in an American high school. I call that a recipe for desperation. But she daily navigated those stormy waters with a calm that could only have come from the Prince of Peace.

Most nights I watched her take the keys and a few worship CDs out to our clunky, old Ford van. She'd climb inside and stay sometimes for hours. (Come to think of it, it's a small miracle the battery never died.) I learned from Atiya. She instinctively understood exactly what her soul needed to be at peace in circumstances that were anything but peaceful. She needed to worship the one, true God.

Like Atiya, I had a God-given instinct that directed me to the source of real peace early on. I became like a blood-hound, spending hours in the Word of God, hunting for God's thoughts about my daily life. I saturated my mind with the Bible so that I gradually experienced the renewal process described in Romans 12:2: "Do not be conformed to this world, but be transformed by the renewal of your mind, that by testing you may discern what is the will of God, what is good and acceptable and perfect."

It's interesting that the Word was so central from the beginning of my walk with Jesus, because Islam does not identify him with a book. Jesus, to most Muslims, is not closely associated with the Bible because he did not write it. Moses wrote a book. Muhammad wrote a book. But not Jesus. Holy books, including the New Testament, are important to Muslims, but they do not understand that Jesus is not only described in the Word; he is, himself, *the Word*. As a former Muslim, I was learning more about this Jesus I followed by studying his book, a book I now understood was not only about him; it was written by him—by his Holy Spirit. This Jesus consistently, stubbornly refused to limit himself to my expectations, which made getting to know him an unfolding adventure of epic proportions.

THE BOOK AND THE LAMB

Muslims consider Jesus one among many prophets. In Islam, each prophet has his own shtick. Jesus is the miracle guy. He is known for healing people, and they respect him for that. Muhammad is the book guy. When I meet Muslims, it's usually a safe bet that they have put Jesus in a miracle box. But no box can hold our Lord. I often challenge Muslims to look for him outside of their normal assumptions about him, to let him out of the box.

Not long after the rest of my siblings came to Christ, I had several opportunities to share my story with the FCA group at Clemson University. One warm, spring night—I think it was my second of three times to speak there—close to two thousand students gathered in the outdoor amphitheater on campus. I stood on the stage with a stately palisade curved behind me, feeling a little like Paul at the Areopagus, mostly because of the physical setting, but also because of the crowd of college students who, like the Athenians, "would spend their time in nothing except telling or hearing something new" (Acts 17:21).

After the event was officially over, most of the students milled around, some asking questions. A guy approached me, and I immediately noticed that he didn't look like he belonged with these clean-cut American kids. He looked more like me.

"Hey, what's going on here?" he asked.

I could tell by the way he assessed the crowd that he'd just arrived and had not heard my talk. "It's an FCA meeting," I told him, "you know, a Christian thing."

"I heard there's a former Muslim guy here."

"Really?" I said. "That would be me. I'm the guy."

I don't remember exactly what he said then, but it was clear he was shocked because he expected the "Muslim guy" to be a black American. It turns out he was from Bangladesh, and he was very curious about why a large group of American students would come to hear what a former Muslim Pakistani from Kuwait had to say. We talked as the crowd dissipated, and I told him I would love to continue the conversation. He also wanted to keep talking, so we went to the closest Waffle House. The place was packed with FCA students who had been at the meeting. I was no stranger to Clemson FCA by then, so I greeted some of the people I recognized as my new friends and we made our way to a booth.

"Mind if I smoke?" he asked.

I told him I didn't. With that formality out of the way, I told him my story. He took it all in, but I could tell he wasn't buying it. He didn't think I was lying, he told me, but he wondered how I could reconcile the many differences that existed between Islam and Christianity. We had a lively discussion as he fired questions at me and I did my best to answer them. For a Muslim, particularly a Sunni Muslim, it always comes back to the book. Christians are known for translating and retranslating the Bible. This is abhorrent to most Muslims because they work hard to keep the Qu'ran pure. If you've ever met someone who is obsessed with a belief that the King James Bible is the *only* reliable translation of the Bible, you get the idea. Muslims respect their book in a way most Christians can't comprehend. They make sure the Qu'ran is never lower than any other book in their homes, and they would never, ever throw it down on a table or couch or write notes in its margins.

I knew I could not sway my Bangladeshi friend by talking about the Bible. In fact, there are verses in the New Testament that would close the door on our conversation if I so much as mentioned them. The old standby, John 3:16, is not a great place to start in a conversation with a Muslim. They will typically shut down at the first mention of Jesus as the Son of

God. To a good Muslim, that sounds like blasphemy because it implies that God had a wife. How else could he have a son? I knew better than to start there. But I did know something we could both agree on.

Sin.

Muslims get sin. That's why they pray five times a day and fast at Ramadan. They follow a strict moral code in order to keep their sins in check. Some Shiites even flog themselves because of their own sins and the sins of others. Muslims also get the connection between sin and blood. Growing up, like many Muslims, my family sacrificed animals for our sins. Once my parents even sacrificed my pet chicken. I was a little bitter about that, but I got over it. If we felt the need to make a better sacrifice, we'd combine resources with other families and buy a bigger animal. The guy sitting across from me at Waffle House understood this idea. The bigger the sacrifice, the more sins and for more people it could atone. So I asked him, "What kind of sacrifice would be big enough for the entire human race?

"Only a God-sized sacrifice," I said in answer to my own question.

I knew I had his attention then. "Forget about Jesus being the Son of God for a minute. Think about him as the Lamb of God. That's who Jesus is, man."

I could tell my words made an impression on him. He didn't stop and kneel on the dirty, tile floor of the Waffle House and accept Jesus right then and there, but he was rattled. Rattling can be a good thing. It can be the first step toward eventual, radical faith. I have no idea what happened to him, but I pray he knows the truth about Jesus now and has chosen to follow him.

On the Attack

I was now heavily involved in the leadership of FCA. I'd moved on from the Baptist church and had become a professional church-hopper. That doesn't mean I was rootless—far from it. In some ways, these years planted a seed in me that grew into the church I planted seven years ago, called Mosaic. I began to see the body of Christ as a multi-gifted, multi-ethnic, multi-style, multi-everything entity. I eventually settled at Seacoast Church, where I saw with more clarity this beautiful, colorful picture of the church. In chapter 8 I'll unpack some of the dirtier laundry from these years of church and ministry (who doesn't have some of that?), but for now I was learning to give away what had been given so freely to me. The Lord opened up plenty of conversations with Muslims, and I was learning how to tell my story more and more effectively.

I was beginning to understand more fully the words Jesus said to me: *Your life is not your own.* But this wasn't just about ownership; it was about purpose. He wanted to use me, to send me to do his work in the lives of people who needed to know him. I was a long way from knowing what that purpose would look like, but I trusted that God would show me in time.

Waging War Against the Enemy

In the meantime I was also learning more about the Holy Spirit. Spiritual warfare wasn't just some weird attack against me that led to my salvation. I was beginning to understand that it was more than that. It was intense, hand-to-hand combat that I was called to fight on behalf of others. My purpose in life was not to wow people with my little story and call it a day. In fact, it was rarely about me at all.

Six of us lived in a little three-bedroom apartment. Just like in Kuwait, we couldn't help but get to know our neighbors. One day Obea knocked on my bedroom door and told me the two girls who lived next door were there and needed to see me. The two girls, one a teenager Atiya's age and the other a few years younger, lived with their parents. As far as we knew, none of them were believers.

"They want you to pray for their apartment," Obea said.

I was about to leave for work, so I told Obea I was in a hurry and couldn't do it.

"But you need to go," she insisted. "They say there's a ghost in their apartment."

"Are you kidding me?" I said, thinking I didn't have time for little girls' silly superstitions.

"Seriously," Obea said, "you need to get over there."

I'm not sure why I took Obea's word for it, but I followed her next door. They had this dog that was normally so calm it was almost comatose, and I could hear it barking like crazy before we opened their door. That was my first clue that something strangely out of the ordinary was going on. I told the youngest daughter to take the dog out for a walk. Before she left, she looked behind me and said, "There! It just went into the bedroom. I saw it."

Her sister explained: "It's a small, white creature that follows us from place to place wherever we move."

Normally by this point I'd start singing "Who you gonna call?" and make a joke about green slime, but I didn't. I was still a very young Christian. I knew maybe five verses from the Bible, tops. Obea was—and is—actually a lot more mature than me even though she is younger. But as I stepped into the apartment, I immediately sensed that the Holy Spirit was on me, and I knew right away that this was about something bigger than a "ghost." I've learned that when it comes to the supernatural, this is usually the case. Sometimes spiritual warfare is a smoke screen for something else. We get so fixated on bizarre circumstances that we miss Jesus and his reason for engineering the circumstances in the first place.

I didn't want to miss the real action, so I began to pray silently, *Jesus, what do you want? What are you doing here?*

Then I said out loud to the girl, "Does this thing bother you?"

"Oh, yes," she answered.

I asked her about her family and about any knowledge of God they might have. Was there any history there? Did they pray or read the Bible? Did they ever go to church? No, not that she'd ever remembered. I knew then that my reason for being there wasn't just to drive out a demon; it was to introduce this girl and her family to Jesus. I shared the gospel with her in simple and direct terms, and she listened intently. Then I said, "Do you want to accept Jesus? Are you willing to pray with me right now? I can pray about the ghost, but the real issue here is Jesus. Do you want to know him?"

She said this was exactly what she wanted to do, so I said, "Let's go into the bedroom and pray," thinking, *We're going to do this right in front of the "ghost."*

The three of us went into the girl's bedroom. Along one wall a bunch of old dolls leaned against one another in a haphazard line. Under other circumstances, that huddled mass of dolls would have still been a little creepy. But as we passed by, I could have sworn one of them turned its head and looked at me. I kept my back to it, but I sensed a presence behind me. I recognized that presence, but now I knew who had authority over it. We prayed together and as soon as my neighbor echoed my "Amen," the phone rang. I motioned to her to go ahead and answer it, so she left the room. I then turned to face the doll, looked directly at it, and said, "You have to leave. Now."

"No I don't," it communicated back to me.

I stepped closer to it and said, "In the Name of Jesus, yes you do."

Obea looked at me like I was crazy, and I saw something I can't begin to describe shooting out of the room, hurling threats and insults back at me as it went. The girl came back in the room, and Obea asked her who had called.

"No one," she said. "They hung up."

Clearly, the Lord was in charge of this encounter, orchestrating every detail. This impressionable, young girl needed to be out of the room so I could do serious battle with the enemy that had plagued her family for so long. With that out of the way, I knew it was time to deliver the message the Holy Spirit had given me, the one I knew was more important than anything else. We walked back into the kitchen, and I said, "I have a message for your mom."

By this time, she was all ears. "Tell your mom it's time to forgive the church. It's time to come back."

I did not know her mom's story. I didn't know anything about her history with the church. It was clear to me that every action, every thought, every word from the moment we left our apartment was from the Lord, not me. I wrote down some information about Seacoast, the church Obea, Mahmood, and I were by this point heavily involved in, and we left.

If the story ended there, it would still be a good one. But I love it when God lets us in on the rest of the story, when it all unfolds in a beautiful validation of Philippians 1:6: "And I am sure of this, that he who began a good work in you will bring it to completion at the day of Jesus Christ." The very next Sunday our neighbors showed up at Seacoast—the whole family. The next time we held a baptism, they were all baptized.

The mom was very transparent about their story, including the "ghost" that "haunted" them, although I'm fairly certain she eventually understood exactly what it was, who sent it, and, best of all, who evicted it from their home. One day, months or maybe even a year later, I overheard a conversation between her and another woman at our church:

"Did that thing ever come back?"

"No, not since the day Naeem came over and prayed."

That made me feel good, but overhearing an accolade in passing doesn't make my day. It's knowing that I did not do anything but access the awesome power of the Holy Spirit. Jesus, as he does over and over again, sought out an entire family and used whatever means available to him—including frightening stuff and an immature, young guy like me—to draw them to himself. Now *that's* a miracle only he can do.

I feel a little foolish telling you this, but after this episode I earned the nickname "Ghostbuster" at Seacoast. And I admit that foolish is exactly how I feel sometimes when I share my story. It sounds so crazy. But I've decided listening to the Holy Spirit is worth it. The gifts of the Spirit are not reserved for the elite or the spiritually mature, and they weren't given to us to make us superheroes. You don't have to be special to get the gifts, because you are already special to God.

The apostle Paul said, "Now about the gifts of the Spirit, brothers and sisters, I do not want you to be uninformed" (1 Cor. 12:1 NIV). Ignorance of God's gifts is just plain sad. That's because our gifts are tied to our purpose. They are the resources God gives us to do the things he asks us to do. For instance, what if God wants me to give, but I don't realize that giving is itself a gift of the Holy Spirit? It will feel like a chore, not a delight. Or what if I have keen insight into the spiritual needs of others, but don't realize God has given me the gift of prophecy or exhortation? I may not act on this insight other than to criticize.

One of the most tragic passages in Scripture is that moment in Matthew 7:21 when Jesus says, "Not everyone who says to me, 'Lord, Lord,' will enter the kingdom of heaven, but the one who does the will of my Father who is in heaven." In the final analysis, I want to learn how to listen to the Holy Spirit and follow his lead, because I've observed that you can live your entire life and miss him. And if that's the case, you are not the only one who misses out. Your friends—the ones who not only want but desperately need the good stuff that comes from opening up the gifts of the Holy Spirit—will miss out too.

SEVEN

BOLLYWOOD
ASPIRATIONS

Christianity is a statement which, if false, is of no
importance, and, if true, of infinite importance.
The one thing it cannot be is moderately important.

—C. S. LEWIS

ONE THING I DIDN'T MENTION about my friend Arvind is
that most of what I understand about the Hindu religion and
culture comes from the time I spent in his home and in the
homes of our other Indian neighbors in Kuwait. Kuwait is,
depending on your source of information, 85 to 95 percent
Muslim. But in my part of the country, in my neighborhood
and my schools in Kuwait City, it was also heavily Hindu. My
Indian neighbors and I loved one another, and like most kids
we didn't think the differences between us were a big deal.
Even with its tacit caste system, Kuwait City was a melting

pot. At the time 60 percent of the people living there were foreign immigrants. Kuwait was where I learned to love diversity.

When I was just a twelve-year-old kid, I crashed my first Indian wedding. A friend of mine who was, unlike me, there as an invited guest had a video camera. It was a big, clunky contraption, outweighing today's sleek, compact cameras like the first car phones compared to a smartphone. I begged him if I could use it, and, against his better judgment, he said yes. Pretty soon, I locked the viewfinder on a pretty girl and started following her around. I felt invisible behind the camera lens. One man noticed me after a while and tapped me on the shoulder. He said (insert my best Indian accent here), "What are you doing?"

To which I wanted to say, "What are *you* doing?"

"Listen to me," he said. "I see what you are doing, and it is not right. I want you to do the video straight. Right?"

I had no idea what he was talking about, but I nodded semi-respectfully, put the camera back up to my face, found the girl, and continued following her around, filming her every move. Again, a tap on the shoulder.

"I know what you are doing, and it is not good."

Again, I nodded. Keeping the girl in sight, I went to my friend and asked, "Who is that guy?"

"Naeem," he said, "that girl you're following around . . . he's her dad."

Apparently everyone knew what I was doing, and he was right, it was not good after all. No more hiding behind a camera for me. But I'll admit it; there was a time when I dreamed of becoming a Bollywood movie star. Have you ever seen one? If you have, you don't blame me, I'm sure.

Living in close proximity to Indian culture influenced me in other, more positive ways too. One of the benefits of a diverse culture is the education that takes place normally, organically, when very different cultures overlap in everyday life. We had many Indian friends, so I learned about their culture naturally in the context of those relationships. Yes, I came from a Muslim family, but that didn't stop me from visiting my neighbors' homes every fall to celebrate *Diwali*, the Hindu festival of lights. I have fond memories of sharing sweets with my friends' families and the warm glow of the special clay lamps Hindu families light in their homes during *Diwali*. These lights symbolize, for Hindus, inner light or an infinite, pure spirituality they call the *tman*. I didn't pay attention to that part of it all, but what boy wouldn't want in on a festival that included fireworks? I also loved the *Holi* festival in the spring and *Raksha Bandhan* that celebrates the love between brothers and sisters.

Most of what I know about Hinduism I didn't learn in textbooks, at least not at first. I experienced it in the homes of my friends and neighbors. Hinduism is so complex that it isn't practiced the same in every region of the world, so let's cover the basics.

Now that I am a follower of Jesus, I understand the fundamental differences between Hinduism and the message of the gospel. But back then my worldview did not acknowledge these differences. I assumed what so many still do, that although we all approached him on vastly different paths, we all worshipped the same God. There are nine core beliefs in the Hindu religion, but these five are the most central:

The Definition of God

Like us, Hindus believe in a trinitarian god—three gods in one. But unlike us, this belief is not only polytheistic it is pantheistic in that they believe nature and god are one and the same. You may hear that Hindus worship millions of gods, and this is why. Just about anything can be a god. The Hindu "trinity" consists of Brahma, Shiva, and Vishnu. You've probably heard of these three. To a Hindu, all other gods—and there are many of them—are offshoots of either Brahma, Shiva, or Vishnu.

The Caste System

Not all Hindus practice it, but many of them believe in this ancient class structure in one sense or another. According to the caste system, people inherit their ranks in life in categories ranging from the Brahman (the priest class) all the way to the Dalit (literally meaning "ground" or "suppressed" in Sanskrit). This class is responsible for the lowest levels of service in Hindu culture. We deny any notion of this in our own culture, but if you think about it, almost every society has practiced a subtle caste system since the beginning of time, and we're no different. We place higher or lower values on people based on arbitrary measures like appearances or family backgrounds. Jesus defied this kind of thinking over and over with counterintuitive instructions to his disciples, such as this: "When you are invited by someone to a wedding feast, do not sit down in a place of honor" (Luke 14:8).

KARMA

This may be the most familiar of Hindu beliefs to Westerners, one that people of many faiths have adopted as their own. Karma, for some, is simply cause and effect that occurs in nature. But many theistic Hindus believe a supreme being is behind every instance of karma.

REINCARNATION

Not to be disrespectful, but reincarnation is a belief in human recycling. The origins of this belief are obscure. Some say it surfaced first in India; others claim it came from ancient Greece. The basic idea is that when biological death occurs the soul goes to live in another physical body, not necessarily a human one. It is—and I guess this is logical—connected to karma in that the next destination for your soul can be good or bad based on the kind of life you live in your current body.

NIRVANA

Nirvana is the ultimate goal of all Hindus. This word could be translated in our Western world as "salvation." Its literal meaning is "blown out," as in extinguishing a candle. Another Hindi word for nirvana is *moksha*, which means, a "liberation from all worldy ties."[1] The concept of nirvana combines the ideas of liberation and communion with a deity in the afterlife. There are three ways for a Hindu to achieve nirvana. It's kind of like a multiple-choice test, where you can choose your method of getting to nirvana: First is the way of works, based on karma. Second is the way of knowledge, or *jnana*. And, third is the way of devotion, or *puja*.

The Problem with Jesus

One day I called Arvind to tell him I would be devoting an entire sermon to Hinduism the following Sunday, and I figured he might want to listen to it. By this time, I had noticed that Arvind posted scriptures and Christian quotes on Facebook from time to time, so I asked him what was up with that. "Are you reading the Bible now?"

"Yeah, I am."

Arvind is a Hindu. I knew that. If I visited his home, I would probably see gods all over the place. If he had a mantel, it would be weighed down with them, including a statue of Jesus. So I said, "Arvind, you're fascinating, bro. You think all roads lead to the same place. You are so tolerant; you're just fine with everyone being okay. I don't have that gift. I think if someone is gonna be right, then someone is gonna be wrong. There's gotta be something that is absolutely true."

Arvind and I can talk like that now. We eventually resolved the tension of his last visit and are back to a great friendship. We've both grown up a lot since then. He made a few comments, and I added, "There's no doubt there are Hindus and Muslims and people of other faiths who are sincere. All religions do good and want to help people reach salvation or nirvana or whatever you want to call it. They want to help you discover God . . . in nature, inside of yourself . . . Their message—all of them—is the same. 'Let me help you find God.' But Jesus is different. He said, 'I am God, here to find you.' That's what is unique about the gospel."

Arvind is not the first person I've met who doesn't yet see this difference, either because they can't understand it or they don't want to. He is my friend, so it's not all that hard these days to have an intelligent discussion with him about Jesus. But sometimes the person I'm talking to isn't like Arvind. Sometimes the person on the other side of a discussion about this one, primary, huge claim that sets Jesus and his followers apart is a little more intimidating.

Not long ago I had a chat with both a history professor from Davidson College and a former Catholic nun who is now Muslim. I am, I admit it, intimidated by smart people. So here I was sitting next to an officially smart person, and, to make matters a whole lot worse, we were on the radio. And not just some local, hick station; it was NPR. I was nowhere near my comfort zone. But I was there to talk about Jesus, so I got to the point early in the program and said, "The claims of Jesus are very different because he claimed to be God."

"No, he didn't," the professor said, just like that.

"Yes, he did," I answered, thinking, *Is that the best I've got?*

"No," he said with that fake patience adults sometimes use with children, "I've never heard anyone substantiate that claim."

I'd like to say I wowed both the smart guy and the former nun (who was pretty smart too) with my theological genius and my vast knowledge of apologetics, but the conversation moved on and that was that. Not because I always have to have the last word, but because Jesus has ultimate claim to it, I'd like to expand my answer, the answer I didn't get to give on NPR, right here.

I AM

Smart people intimidate us, don't they? How about famous people? And pretty people? Folks with credentials or celebrity status bring out my insecurities, and I think if you're honest, you can relate to that.

We freak out in the presence of human glory, so it stands to reason that heavenly glory might have the same effect. In John 18, there is a historical account in which Jesus reveals his glory by making a clear and stunning claim to be God. I won't take the time here to make the case that the record of the New Testament, especially the gospels, is historically reliable. Do your own research, and you'll discover that it is.

You know the story. Jesus and his disciples, after the Passover meal, gathered in an olive grove to pray. Meanwhile, Judas had secured a posse which included priests and a detachment or cohort of Roman soldiers, scholars say about five hundred of them,[2] who brought "lanterns and torches and weapons" in order to capture Jesus (John 18:3). As they approached Jesus, rather than run away, he took the initiative and asked them, "Whom do you seek?" (v. 4). They told him they were looking for Jesus of Nazareth, and he answered, "I am he" (v. 5). This doesn't sound all that meaningful until you understand that the translators added "he" to help the phrase make sense in English. What Jesus really said was, "I AM."

And every Jew in the crowd knew exactly what that meant. This claim to be "I AM" is what got Jesus crucified. He might as well have said, "You know Jehovah, the God who met Moses in the wilderness at a burning bush and told him his name was I AM? The God of Abraham, Isaac, and Jacob? That's me."

What interests me most is how the crowd reacted, including the entire detachment of tough, daunting Roman soldiers. They "drew back and fell to the ground" (v. 6). Even the most intimidating people in the civilized world were intimidated by this claim and the man who made it. Jesus asked them who they were looking for again, and they repeated their answer. Once again, Jesus said, so there could be no mistake this time, "I AM" (v. 8).

Take a minute to think about what just happened. Jesus clearly asserted that he was God, and when he did a group of five hundred Roman soldiers fell to the ground. We're not talking about a bunch of teenage girls at a Justin Bieber concert. It would be like Seal Team Six or Delta Force 5 trembling when one scrawny preacher says two words. There is no doubt that this was a divine, powerful moment. It reminds me of the time Jesus told the Pharisees, "Truly, truly, I say to you, before Abraham was, I am" (John 8:58). In response, the crowd picked up rocks in order to stone him. Again, this is the claim that got Jesus crucified.

If you claim Christianity, you cannot say Jesus is anything but God. And if he is God, all his other claims are true by default. His familiar words, "I am the way, and the truth, and the life," sound exclusive enough as is, but then Jesus adds, "No one comes to the Father except through me" (John 14:6), and you have to accept these words if he is God. Jesus tells us we get into the kingdom through him and him alone, and that he is the "narrow gate" (Matt. 7:13).

Narrow is a negative word; it's hard and uncomfortable. It makes me think of the one and only time I went spelunking. If you're at all claustrophobic, you don't want to be anywhere near a cave, much less crawling through one. If you don't like wet places, pitch-black darkness, or unrecognizable spiders, you should probably stay away from caves too. We were already in a dark, tight spot when our guide pointed to an impossibly small opening and said, "If you can handle it without freaking out, slide through that crack, and you'll be amazed what you find on the other side. But don't try it unless you're up for it because you could get stuck."

It scared me to death, but it sounded like a dare to me, and I can't back down from those. I decided to go for it. And I wasn't sorry.

It was hard and wet and frightening and . . . narrow. But when I finally slid down into the next cave from that tiny gap I wouldn't even call a tunnel, I'll never forget what I saw. A cathedral in middle earth. It felt like the Grand Canyon underground. Narrow was worth it.

Jesus tells us in the same breath that "the gate is wide and the way is easy that leads to destruction" (Matt. 7:13). In other words, broad does not equal freedom. Ultimately all those other options out there (especially the spiritual ones), the ones that seem so appealing, they will suck the life out of you. In the end they will make your life narrow. Jesus, on the other hand, is the only one who offers freedom. "If you live for me alone," he says, "and don't listen to anyone else but me; if you'll get your identity, your opinions, your ideas, your very life from me, I know it seems narrow—it is narrow—but your life will open up to the life you've wanted all along."

The truth is, just like Arvind's, the mantel of my heart is weighed down with other gods that I desperately feel the need to please. It's easy to think of my Hindu friends or my nonreligious friends as the only people with an idolatry problem, but I only have to look as close as my own heart to see how much I am exactly like them. And, to tell the truth, if all I had to go on was Jesus' claim to be God, I'm not sure I could fit my heart into that small space called the gospel. But there's more to the story. With Jesus, there always is.

ME FOR THEM

Back at the grove Jesus said something that reveals him to be God even more distinctly than his out-and-out claim to be the "I AM." This statement reveals more than Jesus' God-identity, it shows us his God-heart. The second time the priests and soldiers told him they were looking for Jesus of Nazareth, he said, "I told you that I am he. So, if you seek me, let these men go" (John 18:8). Legally, the soldiers could have rounded up every follower of Jesus—they probably intended to—and done who knows what to them. But, knowing this, Jesus said, "let these men go." The meaning of these words is enough to knock you down to the ground like a quivering Roman soldier, if you'll let it. He's saying, "Take me for them."

At this point Peter drew his sword and lopped off the high priest's servant's ear. Suddenly, Jesus' plea to let the disciples go must have seemed a little premature. Peter had just become another criminal, a violent one at that, and it's likely they would have taken him too. If I'd been Jesus, I would have appreciated Peter's attempt to fight my enemies. I would have probably been glad to have a coconspirator, someone who would have made prison time and whatever came next a little less lonely. But Jesus, in a beautiful picture of the substitutionary atonement of the cross, replaced the servant's ear and, in his last act of healing on earth, totally erased the crime Peter had just committed. He said, "Put your sword into its sheath; shall I not drink the cup that the Father has given me?" (v. 11).

There's a bigger story here. As it often is, the gospel is embedded in any story where Jesus is at the center. Here's what this story is *really* about:

Jesus was saying,

"I am going to the cross, and you don't have to.

"I'm going to justify you so thoroughly that there will be no evidence of your sin.

"I am going to heal your sins; not just this one, but all of them.

"I'll drink the cup for all of us.

"I'm God, I AM. It's me for all of them."

And here's what I'd like to say to anyone who will listen: could you imagine the greatest love story you've ever heard? In it there is a person who loves you more than any other, who would give everything and anything just to find you. All you need to do is to commit to him, to enter into an intimate, personal relationship with him. I know it seems narrow, but— trust me—in the end, it is as wide as an abundant life on earth and as high as an eternal life in heaven.

EIGHT

CHURCH STORIES

Grace defies reason and logic. Love interrupts, if you like, the consequences of your actions, which in my case is very good news indeed, because I've done a lot of stupid stuff.

—BONO

Like you, I have a personal church history. The timeline of my history may not be as long as yours, but it has more than its share of twists and turns like any good story does. My brother-in-law, Paul, with whom I share a lot of my history and who was my friend long before he even thought about marrying my sister Obea, well, his church history started the day he was born to a Southern Baptist pastor. He's got history—and maybe even some baggage—that stretches farther back than mine.

Maybe you still can't figure out my story. There are too many gaps. How did I go from a foreign college guy hanging out with the Fellowship of Christian Athletes to the pastor of a church called Mosaic? What got me from there to here? What are the epic moments on my timeline after I met Jesus as a new-to-America Muslim fresh from the sands of Kuwait?

Or maybe you're thinking, *Why does it matter? Just get on with it, and tell us some more supernatural stories.* But my life is woven into the larger narrative of the whole body of Christ, just as yours is if you belong to that body, so I can't help but share some of *our* story.

One caveat before I begin: it is not my intention to bash any church, either generally or specifically. The only person I'll bash a little is myself. After you hear some of this stuff, I hope you'll have a good laugh at my expense and even see yourself somewhere in the picture. Maybe your journey is similar to mine. Or maybe you'll see how easily church culture can confuse new believers—especially new believers who come to Jesus from other faiths and other ethnicities. Maybe my experiences will be informative for you as you engage Muslims and welcome them into your community. If nothing else, I hope this is a reminder to never assume everyone's backstory is the same as yours.

But I'm not excusing the church or my part in making church less than it should be either. This very thing—the imperfection of church—has kept my soul on a lifelong search for Jesus. Let's face it. After spending a few months or maybe years in one church, you're going to look around one day and ask, "Is this it?" I contend that one real problem with the church is that most of the people who populate it today are stuck in Christianity. Throughout my short history with the church, I regularly ran the risk of getting stuck the same way. *Wait a minute*, you're thinking, *what's wrong with that? Isn't*

that exactly where we're supposed to be? Stuck in Christianity?
Let me see if I can explain.

SHAKING IT OFF

The first team sport I ever played in the United States was
volleyball. Or, as I called it then, "wallyball." (Ashley still teases
me about that.) Nothing offers more opportunities for cultural
misunderstanding than a team sport. Idioms bounce around
more than the ball. I loved wallyball, but half the time I had
no idea what people were saying on the court. The first time I
spiked a ball, some guy swatted me on the rear. *Wait a minute,*
I thought (and maybe said out loud), *what just happened?*

"That's normal . . . on the court," I was told, "but not anywhere else."

Over and over I'd hear the phrase "shake it off," and I
assumed I knew exactly what it meant. We were playing beach
volleyball, so I figured it was a reminder to dust the sand off
your shorts. Eventually I figured out what "shake it off" meant.
Get over it. Leave the bad experience behind. Move on.

I've been "shaking off" Christianity for years and replacing
it with a genuine pursuit of Jesus. The word *Christian* is used
in the New Testament exactly three times, and even then it is
not used by the disciples but by other people as a slur against
them. It means "little Christ," and that's not such a bad label,
but I prefer *Christ follower* or *disciple,* more accurate biblical
labels that remind me to be accountable to the gospels, to the
kind of life, values, and behavior Jesus modeled and preached
instead of to the arbitrary mores of church culture. I don't

advocate shaking off church, but I do suggest leaving behind the culture of church—a culture that doesn't always rightly represent Jesus. And I have come to insist that we, as individuals and as a body, make pursuing intimacy with God our primary goal. A. W. Tozer said that "the whole transaction of religious conversion has been made mechanical . . . Christ may be 'received' without creating any special love for Him in the soul of the receiver."[1] If that's the case, shouldn't we shake off the mechanical aspects of church and religion to make room for the organic and the intimate, for our rituals and traditions to be replaced with genuine love?

My church history is worth sharing because it highlights how patient and kind God has been with me in this process. I have a feeling your process has baggage and wounds and missteps in it just like mine does. I also know that if you picked up this book, there is something in your core that is searching to know God—maybe even to follow him. And I'm here to tell you his kindness leads us to repent, and his love leads us to change. Even when we get it all wrong. Especially when we get it all wrong.

From day one I was committed to following Jesus, but I did not have a firm grasp on the concept of God's grace. I continued to interact with him on the basis of my performance. I remember the first time I read the Sermon on the Mount and realized my thoughts mattered to Jesus, not just my actions. I was not only shocked; I figured I was sunk. How could God accept me if he not only examined my behavior but scrutinized the inside of my head as well? Slowly I began to know and embrace the kindness of God. Contrary to my first understanding, the kindness I'd experienced when I first met him was not the result of a do-it-once thing. Following Jesus involves whole-hearted, everyday repentance to which he responds every single time with grace. Threaded throughout my personal church history is a slow dawning in my heart that God's grace is accessible every minute of every day, not only when I have a dramatic experience.

Maybe this performance-driven understanding of the Christian faith is why it took me a full year to be baptized, even though I knew it was in some way a part of the deal long before then. Mahmood and others informed me that baptism was something Christians did. I listened to sermons about it. Then I read about it for myself. Why didn't I jump in the water right away? I guess I felt that baptism would legitimize my decision once and for all, that my identity—an identity I'd already compromised a lot by meeting Jesus—would be lost forever. I knew Jesus, but I wondered if I knew him well enough to commit with this kind of finality. One day I stood on the beach watching the pastor of my Baptist church perform baptisms in the surf. After he was done and the event was over, he walked up to me and said, "I hear you want to be baptized."

No! I thought, *I don't. I bet Moody put him up to this.*

But out loud I said I was thinking about it. We talked some more, and I knew then that it was time. I had to fully let go of who I was to become who Jesus wanted me to be.

Over time, I began to understand that God wanted more than my compliance to a new set of rules and rituals. He wanted me to become the person I truly wanted to be, to grow me in fruit and character. He wanted to give me my heart's deepest desire—to make me into a man who is defined by the fruit of the Spirit, who produces lasting fruit in others. These things can never be the product of a to-do list. Ultimately, we don't learn them in a seminar or a sermon series or even a seminary class. They are grown in us, not by us. And God often grows them in us by using imperfect Christ followers in the very imperfect church.

AMATEUR CHURCH-HOPPER

I've already mentioned that at times some people dismissed my story and told me I had had a dream, not a real experience. Maybe it was easier for them to digest it that way. But those same people usually felt compelled to straighten out my theology too. I didn't even know what the word *theology* meant, so I figured I should listen to them since they must be the experts. Surely I didn't understand sin, they told me. Surely I hadn't used the right words to ask forgiveness for that sin. This is why I prayed the "sinner's prayer" so many times. I had been introduced to Jesus, but this thing called salvation and all the stuff that went with it was in a completely different category. It was like Area 51, a no-man's-land of secrets. Eventually I began to crave a church where the Jesus I was getting to know better every day was clearly present. And it would be nice if that church would help me make sense of everything else.

I went to Bible studies right off the bat. But I had no idea what was going on there. My only experience with a spiritual book was the Qu'ran and the Hadith, a collection of the sayings of Muhammad. In fact, most of what you see practiced in Islam comes from the Hadith. I assumed the Bible was one big, long, holy book; or maybe, like our Islamic books, two books, the Old and New Testaments. When the leader said, "Open to the book of John 17:1–3," I thought I could get there via a page number, so I'd ask what page it was on and people would help me out, but not before shaking their heads like, *Poor Naeem, he thinks we're all on the same page.* Apparently, this Bible thing was more complicated than I thought. There were sixty-six books. Who knew?

I started out at the Baptist church where a lot of my new Fellowship of Christian Athletes friends went. FCA was a campus ministry, but it was heavily populated and led by people who went to this one particular church. Paul and I began to wonder if we shouldn't try some other churches. I was on a hunt to find a church that reflected the Jesus I'd met, the one I was reading about in the New Testament, the one who seemed a little wild and never boring. I felt that there must be more to following him than what I was learning in a traditional church. Paul was on what may have been a more significant journey. All he had ever known was the Baptist church. He desperately wanted something more, something different and powerful.

And so the two of us, along with a handful of friends, became a little band of church vagabonds. First we visited an Episcopal church, followed by just about every variety of church we could find around Charleston. I don't think we were very scientific about it; we just visited random places. Meanwhile, Paul and I were still involved at FCA. He became the president of our chapter, and I helped him lead. What we lacked in skill and maturity, we made up for in passion.

First Stop: Charismania

I've already mentioned my friend Pastor Satish. The first Sunday Paul and I and a few other friends from FCA went to his charismatic church in Columbia, I thought, *Now that's what I'm talking about!*

Something big and God-sized appeared to be going on there. It wasn't predictable like the Baptist church. I never knew what was going to happen next. It felt dangerous, in a good way. It wasn't stuffy and controlled—far from it. *Wow,* I thought, *when the Holy Spirit moves the pastor, his voice even changes.*

That first Sunday, I took a big gulp of the Kool-Aid. And I kept on drinking it. Someone gave me a Dake Bible, often dubbed the "Pentecostal Bible," which included a bold commentary that assured believers of guaranteed prosperity and health, and I just ate it up. "Name it and claim it" was a good thing, apparently. You just had to have faith in your faith. I discovered Benny Hinn, and I thought he was the jam! I decided to become a faith healer and travel the globe. There was a heavy emphasis on getting a "word from the Lord," or listening in prayer in order to hear a specific phrase from him—something personal that was meant to encourage or exhort others. So I prayed for words, and sometimes I got them. Older men in the congregation would pray over us, and there was intense pressure to speak in tongues or fall out on the carpeted floor or give some other supernatural evidence of the Holy Spirit. The gift of tongues was considered the supreme proof of a person's salvation.

The first few times a leader prayed over me, nothing happened. Then, one day, a pastor simply said, "Tongues of fire" over me, and the Lord unlocked something in the deepest part of my heart. I not only spoke in tongues; I began to experience more of the Holy Spirit. To this day I'm still not totally sure which of these experiences were real and which were not, but at the time I was certain every bit of it was authentic. I continue to have a lot of respect for Pastor Satish. He is a godly man, and I can never thank him enough for his influence on my growth during this time of my life.

And yet I was beginning to realize that what I thought was unscripted was just as predictable—in a very different way—as the Baptist church. Not every expression of the Holy Spirit was in fact the Holy Spirit. It's not like anyone was faking—far from it. It's just that, like every church, this one wasn't perfect. But this was a slow dawning.

We didn't break our ties with the Baptist church. In fact, our little band of friends ministered every chance we got. We led a series of revival meetings at a rural Baptist church not far from Charleston that happened to be Paul's father's church. I'm sure they still wonder what hit them that weekend—I'm not saying God didn't work or that we were not effective ministers. That very weekend I preached my first sermon, and, according to Ashley's notes, it wasn't all that bad.

In the meantime Paul and I remained leaders at FCA. Our leadership prayer meetings before the big group meetings got really lively. We prayed in tongues; we asked God for crazy things, claiming them actually, and everyone else freaked out. Let me say it clearly: we were young and we were dumb. We led like a freight train, unheeding of how we were confusing and even misleading the people in our path. Something needed to be done about us, and it wasn't long before it was.

What happened next was classic overkill, but in the long run it turned out for our good.

The faculty sponsor, backed by the Baptist church that many FCA people still attended, presented a formal document to us. This paper said, in so many words, that we would not talk about the Holy Spirit. They asked us to sign it. I honestly don't believe these men and women were skeptical of the Holy Spirit as they were of our maturity and leadership. I would never recommend this kind of ultimatum though.

Paul refused and resigned as president. So did I.

This was my first encounter with church conflict, and it wasn't much fun. But what came out of it was life altering. It didn't go down as much like the Inquisition as it sounds. The leaders who drafted the document did a very wise thing. They brought both sides of the issue together with a mediator, a man who became a major influence in my life and remains one of my friends and heroes to this day.

The School of Michael Morris

I call him the Gentle Giant. Michael Morris was on staff at Seacoast Church (and still is) when someone in FCA decided he would bring a balanced view to the table in our meetings to discuss the division Paul and I had created in the leadership. Like Paul, Michael had grown up in a Baptist church. Like both of us, he had swung far to the other side as a younger man. I immediately saw something in this man—who literally towered over the rest of us, since he is at least six foot nine—something I wanted in my own life. I don't know if it was balance (I wasn't exactly looking for that at the time) or that I simply saw Jesus in him, but I asked him if he would mentor me, and he said he'd pray about it.

After a few days he agreed to meet with me, and for the next three years Michael and I had lunch together once every week. I told him everything, including my plans for the faith healer gig. He said something to me that I still remember fifteen years later: "Naeem, I think you need to let your vision die so God can resurrect his in you."

Given my theology at the time—a mind-set that placed far too much emphasis on *my* faith, *my* visions, and *my* words—that sounded like heresy. At first. I thought, *That settles it; this is our last meeting. You're an idiot.* But I kept going to lunch with him. Now you see why I cite the kindness of God as the main theme of my personal church history. Time and time again, God overrode my immaturity and arrogance. He took me by the hand, using men like Paul, Pastor Satish, Michael Morris, and Greg Surratt, the pastor at Seacoast, and he fashioned me into a more mature man than I could have possibly become without their influences.

Michael invited me to a First Wednesday Service at Seacoast. Unlike their seeker-sensitive services on Sundays that were designed to appeal to the nonbelievers and the nonreligious, this service was geared toward feeding and equipping believers. I thought it was so watered down. In my vocabulary, *laid-back* and *Spirit-filled* were exact opposite terms. The singing was great, but when was it going to go a little crazy?

But I kept going back. I remember telling Greg Surratt that I was going to be on staff at Seacoast. Just like that. He looked at me and said, "Well, let's see what God does." Later, as a junior in college, I sought Greg's advice. Should I transfer to a Bible College and then go on to seminary? Greg told me, "Honestly, what you really need is on-the-job training, and seminary won't give you that. Finish college and continue to serve here. Do the best you can. Learn. Lead." Then again he added, "And let's see what God does." This time I got the point.

Michael did far more than go to lunch with me. God had called me to a life of ministry, but Michael understood that the endgame of this calling should remain a mystery for the time being. Even so, he knew that whatever ministry ended up looking like in my life, I would need some basic skills. He took me along with him to minister at bedsides and grave-sides. He allowed me to lead the men's ministry with him. He coached me and then gave me other young men to coach. He taught me a balanced view of the spiritual gifts—one that did not deny or avoid them, but didn't enthrone them either. Maybe more than any other man in my life, Michael Morris grew me up.

He encouraged me to read and dive into deeper, richer books than I'd read before, like *The School of Christ* by T. Austin Sparks, *Passion for Jesus* by Mike Bickle, and *Imagine Meeting Him* by the African pastor Robert Rasmussen. Michael is a tough guy, but he is tender as well. He is a stickler for passion for Jesus. According to Michael, this passion is the only foundation for real leadership. This—the centrality of a deep, abiding love life with Jesus—is what I traded in my "name-it-and-claim-it" theology for. I've never regretted it.

I learned from Michael, and from these godly authors of old, that imitating Jesus is not the same as allowing him to live his life inside me and through me. Christianity may be objective, but following Jesus is subjective. As T. Austin Sparks says:

> I'm quite sure many of you will immediately discern that
> is just the flaw in a very great deal of popular Christianity
> today—a kind of objective imitation of Jesus which gets
> nowhere, rather than the subjective learning of Jesus which
> gets everywhere.[2]

One other thing happened that totally devastated my belief that I could tell God exactly what to do and he would do it every time just because I said it. Something that squashed my confidence in "name it and claim it" once and for all. Ashley, my future wife, broke up with me.

NINE
ASHLEY'S STORY

*Do not stir up or awaken love until the appropriate
time.*

—Song of Solomon 8:4 HCSB

I KISSED DATING GOOD-BYE LONG before Joshua Harris
wrote the book by the same title. But Ashley didn't get that
memo, so at first she wondered what took me so long to ask her
out. Suffice it to say it's a miracle we got together at all. But I'm
getting ahead of myself.

Ashley was born in the South to two Southern parents.
If you're from the South, you understand that she inherited
a distinctive, Bible-Belt identity—one that is imbedded as
deeply inside of her as my Middle Eastern ethnicity is in me.
Fried okra and grits, church more than once a week, the lake
in the summer and hardly any snow in the winter. She lived
in Greenville, South Carolina, in upper-middle-class suburbia,
where the Gulf War was far away in the realm of television

news, and Islam belonged in *Arabian Nights* more than it did in Ashley's neighborhood. Her church background is a mixture of Presbyterian and traditional Southern Baptist. Pretty standard for a Southern girl. From the outside, her home looked idyllic, and in some ways I guess it was. But swimming in the undercurrent beneath her average-American home life were some murky waters too—complicated issues she was too young to understand at the time.

By the time Ashley graduated from high school she was ready to get out of there. So she packed up and left for college in Charleston with a sense of relief, along with a boatload of insecurities. She knew Jesus and had known him since childhood. She was "saved" in that elusive, cultural sense I mentioned earlier. She had a genuine, although immature, relationship with Jesus, but she had no idea how much she was missing.

Ashley and I were no more than faces in a crowd to each other at first. Both of us were involved in FCA, but it was a large group, so our paths didn't cross all that often during my first two years in Charleston. She was a Spanish major and spent the first half of her junior year at the Universidad de los Andes in Mérida, Venezuela. It was an extremely hard season for her. Thankfully, as difficult experiences can, this one served to drive her toward God in a new way. We got reacquainted when she came back to finish her junior year. Then, in her senior year, Ashley started going to Seacoast Church, and several months later I started attending there too. This put us in contact with each other all the time. Ashley had also developed a close friendship with Obea by this point. Before long she and I were hanging out . . . a *lot*.

We Kissed Dating Hello

Ashley would have called it dating, but I had a different take on things. I felt dating would be an encumbrance to my growth as a believer. Early on in my faith walk, before I met Ashley, I had decided I would not date at all for three years. It was mighty convenient that our "hanging out" together occurred at the end of that three years. But even then I was skeptical of dating. I made a decision that I would not date anyone unless I could do it with marriage in mind. So at first Ashley and I didn't date; we hung out, as I said already, a lot.

Eventually, after praying about it, I told Ashley I wanted to officially date her. I made it clear that I was in this for the long haul. Ashley wasn't so sure about the long-haul part, but she cared enough about me to hang in there for the time being. For Ashley, the traditional dating paradigm was as familiar to her as her high school prom, and that paradigm didn't necessarily result in marriage. Despite the differences in our cultural backgrounds, we meshed very well from the beginning. But our take on dating was one of the ways I was clearly more Middle Eastern and she was more American. My ideas were formulated more by what the Scriptures taught me than by a culture that was only one generation away from arranged marriages, but I'm sure my background had to have influenced me too.

Because I had to work to pay for everything, including books, tuition, and all my living expenses, my college education took a lot longer to complete than Ashley's. By the time she was a senior and close to graduation, I was still slowly, methodically making my way through college. After earning an associate's degree by piecing together my coursework from the College of Charleston and two other community colleges, I scheduled a meeting with the president of the College of Charleston. I all but begged for admittance (well, I *did* beg), and I was accepted, provided I would maintain a B average and would stay in school until graduation. I paid for the rest of my education with whatever work I could find, often working three jobs at a time. I cut grass, sold men's clothing, and even worked a short stint modeling—anything that would pay for school.

Later, after Ashley graduated, she regularly took a good portion of cash from her Friday paycheck at her job in downtown Charleston and walked it straight to the campus registrar's office to "anonymously" add her contribution to my rising tuition bill.

We sort of dated for most of Ashley's senior year, or, if you place it on the timeline from the previous chapter, during the height of my "charismania" phase. I meant well, but I really pestered Ashley about the Holy Spirit. Every chance I got I hounded her to pray with me, so much so that Obea and Ashley often commiserated about how annoying I was. At least Ashley could take comfort in knowing she wasn't the only one on my radar. Even so, she was seeking God, and she knew I had experienced something she wanted. She saw that my life was about more than a sensational story or two. To Ashley, I exhibited a deeper, wilder freedom in God that she longed to have in her own life.

I wasn't the only person who caused Ashley to hunger for the Lord in a new way. Seacoast gave her a startling, new picture of the church. Her first reaction when she visited there was that she had never seen a church like it. It was full of life, and she knew in her soul that the life she'd sniffed out there was not the result of their untraditional worship model; it was the Holy Spirit. The third person of the Trinity was often ignored in the churches she had gone to until then, but she knew he was important—maybe even a key to unlocking her longings for more of the Lord. So she listened to me and even let me pray with her. I remember one night I prayed over her to receive the Spirit, and when we said "Amen" together I looked at her and said, "Sooo? Did anything happen?"

She hated to disappoint me, but she said, "Nooo, sorry."

But God did something that night. It was subtler than what either of us had hoped for, but it was a first step in a process. Ashley is a researcher, so she read everything she could get her hands on about the Holy Spirit. She read Jack Deere's *Surprised by the Power of the Spirit,* and she told me it shook her to her core. She wondered, *Is this real or is it crazy?* She asked questions, dug deeper, and came to the conclusion that the Holy Spirit had power that was accessible to the average believer, like her. She felt she had been living a limited, defeated life. She was full of fear because of her family background and struggled with depression and deep insecurity. One night, she became convinced that God wanted to free her from all that.

FREEDOM

That night she sensed God telling her it was time to throw her Zoloft away. I cannot stress enough that this is *Ashley's* story, not anyone else's. I understand that many, many people rely upon medication, and that is not sin or weakness. It's simply a medical necessity. I do not believe medication, like the Zoloft Ashley was taking at the time, is a faithless alternative. Please understand that this is merely a descriptive account, not a prescriptive one.

That night Ashley went to Paul, who at the time was my best friend and not quite yet Obea's boyfriend, and she asked him to pray over her. She told him she was ready to be free. They prayed, she threw the pills away, and she has never looked back. No side effects and no more depression. From that point on, she began to walk in a new freedom. Ashley's experience was not as emotional or dramatic as mine, but that's because we're such different people, and the Holy Spirit often works in us according to those differences. In the same way, your story may include the filling of the Holy Spirit while also including the healing and counsel and, yes, medication offered by the medical profession.

Meanwhile, Mahmood had gotten more and more serious about a girl he met through FCA at the College of Charleston. Chelle would become his wife before long. During this same time, Chelle's mom, Becky, had begun a college group at Seacoast. Ashley and I both consider our time in this group a major influence on our early spiritual formation. We learned in an intensely loving community what it meant to hear from God for each other, and to speak those prophetic words over one another. We basically used each other as guinea pigs in this experiment called Spirit-led living. Perhaps as a testimony to the kind of bond we developed, three married couples—Ashley and me, Paul and Obea, and Mahmood and Chelle—all moved toward marriage in that group. Our lives are entwined with one another's to this day.

Ashley's family and I connected during this time as well. She called her dad a few days before I visited Greenville to prep him to meet her new boyfriend for the first time. "Dad," she said, "he's kind of dark."

"How dark?" her dad asked, uncharacteristically, because Ashley had never known her dad to have race issues. But she was about to take her dark, possible future husband to visit her Southern, very white family, after all, so she was a little nervous. Any fears she had were unfounded, though. I immediately won her family over, and they won me over too. In fact, Ashley's dad and I now share a father-son bond that began the very first day we met. Today, our relationship with her parents is delightful evidence of what God can do. My in-laws have experienced God's healing grace in ways Ashley never could have imagined back then. But that's their story to tell.

After Ashley graduated she didn't have any set career plans, so she was in many respects a free agent. We were still dating, but marriage was far away on the horizon because I still had so much schooling to finish. During her last years of college, Ashley had entertained the thought that Jesus might want her to do full-time mission work, so when she heard about the Youth With A Mission (YWAM) mercy ships, she decided to sign up for a six-month discipleship training on their Caribbean ship called the *Caribbean Mercy*. She'd been on mission trips to Ecuador before, and she had spent the semester abroad in Venezuela, so she did not expect this transition to be all that difficult. Besides, if she ended up marrying me, a life of missions was to be her fate. She worked the summer after graduation, and then she left me for six whole months. The group sailed for the first three months and spent the second three months in the Dominican Republic. We wrote letters the entire time she was away.

Contrary to what Ashley thought, she was not prepared for those six months. Not even close. During the first three months on the ship, her mission leader attempted suicide. Ashley and another girl found her. *That* wasn't in the guidebook. She was lonely and confused, and, in the final analysis, utterly broken. What strength she thought she possessed was nonexistent. By the time the group got to the Dominican Republic she was beginning to decide that, heck no, she did not want to be a missionary. They stayed in dirty huts with no electricity and tarantulas as big as her hand. I happen to know my wife hates spiders. She was so overwhelmed by the poverty around her and by the fear inside her that she felt useless in the ministry. She was paralyzed.

By the time New Year's Eve rolled around, Ashley had had it with the whole thing. And it was hard not to include me in the "whole thing" called missions. Not that she had it all thought out by then, but she was ready to end things with me—the boyfriend who was still talking about going to India as a faith-healing missionary—because she just couldn't sign on for that kind of life. If missions were where I was going, she definitely couldn't go there with me. The whole experience had done her in, and she later told me she was a spiritual ruin.

So Ashley called and told me we were through. I was stunned. We had been writing back and forth, and I'm pretty sure she'd never mentioned "I'll probably be breaking up with you soon" in any of her letters. I called her back to tell her a prayer group of seasoned, older believers at Seacoast had given me a clear, prophetic word the night before her break-up call to the effect of, "The Lord will give you the desires of your heart."

And, as far as I could tell, that meant Ashley. She told me I could take my prophetic word and shove it.

When her time with YWAM ended, there was no place for her to go but home to Greenville, the last place on earth she wanted to be. Sure, there was electricity and air-conditioning there, and there were no humongous, hairy spiders, but the way she saw it, she was just trading in one set of issues for another. She did *not* want to be there. But because she had no clue where she did want to be, home was her only alternative, so she settled in and hoped to figure it out before she went crazy.

SIX PAKISTANIS AND ASHLEY

Obea and Ashley had remained close friends. One day not long after Ashley had moved back to Greenville, Obea called her. "Why don't you come here for a visit?" she said. "Just talk to Naeem. That's all I ask."

Given her situation at the time, it seemed like an offer that was impossible to refuse. If anything, she needed closure. Our entire family, except for my dad, was living at that time in one three-bedroom apartment: three boys in one bedroom, two girls in another, and my mom in the third. She stayed with the girls for the weekend. That Obea, she's no dummy. The minute Ashley and I saw each other, it was all over. It was a "you-had-me-at-hello" moment, for sure. We went for a walk and decided right then and there to get back together. I told her, "I want to make something clear: if we start dating again, it's all or nothing. We'll get married."

If you think this was the ultimatum of an overbearing, chauvinistic, Middle Eastern man, you'd be wrong. Ashley has said many times that I told her exactly what she needed to hear. She's no pushover, but this time her fear of commitment was vanquished by my certainty, because in her own heart she knew it was time to commit to me and to our relationship.

It didn't take much for my family and me to convince Ashley to move back to Charleston. The only problem was that she had no job and no place to live. She moved into the apartment, bringing the total occupants of that small apartment up to seven. My family welcomed her with open arms, especially Obea, but she couldn't help but wonder how my mom felt about this random white woman sharing her daughter's bedroom. The plan was for her to stay a week or two until she could move into her own place. She eventually got a job and her own apartment with a roommate, but the week or two we all thought it would take turned into four months.

Ashley decided she would need to learn how to cook Pakistani food, so she followed my mom around in the kitchen, asking her a million questions. At that time Mom spoke almost no English, so it was a frustrating process. She would ask Obea or Atiya about some of the spices she used, but they were no better at translating the mysterious ingredients into English. She eventually gave up on cooking Pakistani cuisine.

It's ironic, if you think about it; here she was in close quarters with another culture, not unlike her time in the Dominican Republic that she'd been so eager to escape (well, minus the spiders and the lack of electricity). This total immersion in the life of a Pakistani, former-Muslim family was not a lot different from her earlier culture shock. But this time she was exactly where she was meant to be.

In many ways, my family taught Ashley everything she needed to know about reaching out to Muslims. It's not as complicated as we think it is. My mom does not care how much Ashley knows about the Qu'ran. What she cares about is whether or not Ashley loves her son and her grandchildren. If she is who she says she is. If she loves her. This is a test my wife has passed with flying colors. Ashley lived with my family for a season and then, years later, my parents lived with us for an even longer season. They were in our home for three years, so they got to see our faith in action. They saw our humanness—the good, the bad, and the ugly—and they saw Jesus. Incarnational living, living among people and relating to them intimately, is of far more value than anything an evangelism or apologetics course can teach us. I'm not suggesting we don't learn to understand our Muslim neighbors and friends and coworkers, but I am saying that it is our relationships that matter most. If people don't see the teachings of Jesus lived out in us, they won't want to listen to a word we have to say about him.

We got married two and a half years later, in the fall of 1999. In this interim I finished college, and, I hope, grew into a much more balanced, healthy man spiritually. Ashley grew too. That year I completed an internship with the youth and men's ministries at Seacoast, all the while juggling several other jobs, including stocking merchandise at the Brookstone store in the mall nearby. At the end of my internship I took on the role of middle school ministry director for the time being.

I went from job to job at Seacoast, learning all kinds of ministry skills along the way. Ashley worked as an assistant to another pastor, Sam Lesky, and pretty much followed him as he took on various roles at the church. Sam was more than a boss. He and his wife, Joan, mentored us in our new marriage, offering friendship and valuable role models. Both Ashley and I are all-in people. Even before we were officially on staff there, we slept, ate, and dreamed Seacoast. When our first child, Asher, was born, Ashley remained on staff part-time and just took the baby with her to work. At Seacoast we learned what a community of believers looked like: a group of people doing life together who embraced the great commandment—to love God and to love one another—and the great commission—to love the world enough to share the gospel with its people. It was a sweet life. Ashley loved our little family, she loved Seacoast, and she loved living in Charleston. Change was not on her radar. Until I put it there.

A Dream Called Mosaic

I started talking about planting a church rather early in our marriage, even before we were as rooted as we eventually became at Seacoast. At first, Ashley basically ignored me. There was too much going on in our here-and-now to dream about the future. Besides, being all in, she assumed we would live out the rest of our days at Seacoast, and she would have been delighted to do so. Even when she began paying attention to my comments, she assumed I was daydreaming and it would pass. Or, in her less gracious moments, she thought, *He's crazy.*

Don't get me wrong; when Ashley signed on to live the rest of her life with me, she agreed to follow me anywhere. She trusted me. She was 100 percent onboard for anything, and I mean anything. She even understood that during the brief moments when she wasn't so sure about trusting me, she could trust God enough to follow her husband. But she figured all this talk about planting a church was just that—talk. Maybe she didn't hear it as anything more because she didn't want to leave Seacoast or Charleston, but to her ears it sounded like a bunch of ideas, not an actual plan. Until one day when she finally realized I was serious.

We went to our favorite breakfast-date place in Mount Pleasant, Bagel Nation. Ashley was pregnant with Asher. I looked into her eyes and told her I had something important to say. For the first time she listened intently as I explained what I wanted to do, what God was leading me—which meant us—to do.

"We need to do this," I said, "not right now, but in a couple of years."

And so it was settled. We eventually made the decision to move to Charlotte when the time came. Ash moved to part-time work at Seacoast, and then she quit altogether so we could learn to live on my salary. As I've mentioned, Ashley is a researcher, so she started reading right away. She put together a notebook with all her findings, everything from ethnic demographics to zip codes to church-planting wisdom. Now that it was more than just talk, she was ready for whatever came next.

This dream would have a longer gestation period than a pregnancy, but it was going to happen, and we could trust God to birth it at the right time no matter what happened in the meantime. And, believe me, there were some big meantimes ahead.

TEN

Hope for the Hopeless

And then, on September 11, the world fractured.

—Barack Obama

THERE HAVE BEEN A FEW times in my life when hope seemed like a preposterous notion. But really, what everyone needs most in those times is the very thing we've lost: hope. Hope that God sees us when we are as far away as a human can be from the divine. Hope that he will come for us wherever we are. Hope that he will reveal himself to us. Hope that he is ultimately in control and that his control is ultimately for our good. And, finally, that when we tell others about the hope we have in Jesus, it will sound authentic in their ears. Because it has become authentic to us.

If ever there was a time when I was tempted to lose hope, it was about a year before Ashley and I moved to Charlotte to start Mosaic. That's when my mom left, and I wondered if I'd ever see her again.

Everyone knows that the months following 9/11 were volatile ones here in the States, but I doubt most Americans understand what it was like for the more than thirty million immigrants living here at the time. If your status was undetermined and you were waiting for your day in court, the government told you it was time to go back home and wait in your own country. And who knew when that wait would end? As fearful observers of the uncertainty around us, my family couldn't always make sense of why some people were banned and some were not. What made us most nervous at the Fazal house was the news that anyone who had overstayed their welcome for any amount of time could count on deportation sooner rather than later.

9/11

You'll recall that I got religious asylum just months after arriving here. I'd finally received my green card before 9/11, so I knew without a doubt that I was safe from deportation. Obea had arrived with a student visa, like Mahmood, and because she married when she graduated, she was legal. No gaps in her stay or Mahmood's. Neither of them were citizens, so while they were allowed to live and work here legally, they could not travel outside the country. Dad had almost airtight, secure status as an international businessman. As soon as Mom, Ali, and Atiya arrived, we started strategizing about how we were going to safely and legally keep them here with us.

Our friend Pastor Satish connected us with an immigration attorney, and we met with him to talk about our options. We settled on applying for religious asylum for all three of them. It had worked for me, so why not for them? Atiya and Ali were now believers, and therefore it was not a good idea for them to return to the Middle East. Mom was another story. We figured as a Muslim she could experience repercussions because of her children's faith if she lived in either Kuwait or Pakistan, especially her homeland of Pakistan. At least that's what we decided to tell the judge. It was a long shot, and we all knew it.

The day we were to appear, we left our Charleston apartment in the middle of the night in order to get to Atlanta in plenty of time for our 7:00 a.m. court date. In those days a hotel room was an unthinkable luxury for us. A friend loaned us his car because it was more reliable than our van. It was a big boat of a car, a Lincoln town car or something like that, and we all piled in for our date with destiny. I went along for moral support and to translate if necessary. Obea and Mahmood came too. Somewhere on a barren stretch of I-20, the supposedly more reliable car broke down. It didn't have a flat tire, and it didn't run out of gas. It simply quit working, as in turn the key and absolutely nothing. And then, if there was any doubt that this particular means of transportation was roadkill, the engine began to spew smoke.

A guy who seemed pretty normal and un-serial-killer-like stopped and offered us a ride, but his car wasn't big enough for all of us to fit in. Of course, Atiya, Ali, and my mom got priority status. The attorney wedged in too. The rest of us waited for AAA to tow the car and to arrange a ride to get us to Atlanta. We freaked out because missing this court date would delay the process by six to eight months. Think the DMV hassles times ten.

Somehow we all made it to the courthouse on time, and the

judge heard my brother, my sister, and my mom each present their cases in turn, all backed by our more eloquent attorney. Despite the fact that Ali and Atiya were minors who struggled to answer the judge's questions in the English language, the court granted them asylum. Or maybe it was *because of* those deficiencies. Who knows? When the judge announced their verdicts we felt hopeful, but the feeling was short-lived. They denied my mom. We drove home with mixed emotions, happy to have Atiya and Ali's situations straightened out, but mostly feeling a rising panic about Mom. Our attorney assured us we could appeal, and, within a week, we did. After that, although we had no closure, we were able to keep her case moving along in the legal system, filing and refiling requests, and we felt she was safe for the time being. We quit worrying, and life moved on.

Until 9/11.

We watched the news and listened to the rumors with a sense of foreboding. I remember the day Mom got the letter we had all dreaded but knew would come. She was to report to the immigration office immediately. The authorities had searched back five years and discovered the one-week lapse between Mom's court appearance and her appeal. The deal was, if you overstayed your visa by any amount of time, even a week, you risked deportation for anywhere from three to ten years.

We had a family meeting right away to assess the options, and we brainstormed for hours. By that time I was a citizen, and I thought I could simply sponsor Mom, but this turned out to be impossible. My mentor, Michael Morris, came and prayed with our family. I've never felt more hopeless about a situation in my life. I confess that for a fleeting moment we entertained the possibility of simply ignoring the summons. Then Michael said something that I found difficult to believe with my heart in these circumstances, even though I knew it in my head. His comment represented a turning point for me, and as we continued to discuss the problem, I finally embraced the truth of his words. Michael said, "Your mom's life is much better off in God's hands than in ours."

Trusting God with my mom's future was one of the hardest things I've ever done.

In the end, the US government assigned an immigration officer to my mom who escorted her from Charleston to New York and made sure she got on the plane to Pakistan. It was humiliating for her, and it felt as final as death to all of us. We knew we would not see her for at least three years, possibly many more.

Incognito

At the end of Mom's first year in Pakistan, we all decided someone needed to check up on her in person. During that first year, I had written letters to politicians and anyone else who might have some influence with the immigration authorities, pleading for my mom's return. I'd tried everything I knew to get her home, to no avail. We decided it was time to go to Pakistan to continue our campaign there. I was the only one besides Dad who could leave the country legally. Just to be safe, not knowing how certain his status would be after 9/11, we'd called Dad home later that fall in 2001 and asked him to stay in the States until things settled down. So I was the one to go. It made sense for me, as a US citizen, to visit Mom and see what I could do to get her home from there. Plus, we all desperately wanted first-hand reassurance that she was okay. Ashley and I were in the process of planning our move to Charlotte, so it wasn't convenient, but we all agreed that it was time.

It might have been fun if I weren't so concerned for Mom. I felt like a spy on a secret mission. We decided that no one could know that I was a Christian, much less a pastor. It was too dangerous for Mom. And it was dangerous for me too. If anyone found out I was a *kafir* (infidel), it wasn't likely I'd make it out alive. They couldn't know I was married to an American either, so I took off my wedding ring and flew incognito to Lahore.

As soon as I got on the plane, the sense of adventure was gone and a minor paranoia replaced it. I sat in an aisle seat, with a mountain of a businessman in the middle, and a Muslim girl at the window seat. I could tell she was Muslim because she was completely covered up. None of us spoke. To tell you the truth I was a little afraid to engage in conversations with strangers, especially ones who were obvious Muslims. Proximity to this young woman made me a little uncomfortable, I'm not gonna lie. I was thankful for the huge guy in the middle seat who partially blocked my view of her. I imagined that she would be able to see through my disguise if I said as much as one sentence to her.

Toward the end of the flight, after dinner, my cup of coffee spilled. On a long flight, I generally have stuff tucked in every available space in and around my seat, so my coffee got on my books, my newspaper, everything. I tried to sop it up with the only thing I had, the airline cocktail napkin. Out of the corner of my eye, I saw the girl fluttering a few napkins toward me. I thanked her and took them, hoping she knew enough English to understand my gratitude. The guy in between us was sound asleep.

After I'd pretty much soaked the napkins, I waved them back at her, just to be cute, and said, "Thanks. Want them back?"

She smiled and said, "No, thanks."

Once we each realized the other spoke English, it was almost impossible not to start a conversation. We exchanged a few pleasantries, and, after hearing my name, she said, "Oh, you're a Muslim."

"Yeah," I said, sort of justifying this because I was supposed to be 007, right? But I felt terrible. She asked more polite questions, and I told her I wasn't married, that I was a counselor or something like that. *Why, God,* I wondered, *would you start a conversation here just so I could lie?*

She was Indian, but lived in Dubai. The more we talked, the more we discovered similarities between us. We liked the same Indian movies. Our families were alike. But still I felt bad for deceiving her and for refusing to admit that I was a Christian. Our conversation was still going strong, the guy in the middle still out cold, when the flight attendant announced that we were about to land.

I had over an hour layover, so I took my time heading to the gate for my next flight. I stood on the moving sidewalk, still feeling like a turncoat, and I looked behind me. There she was. It turns out our connecting flights left from the same gate, and she had all the time in the world to chat. *What's going on here, God?* I thought. *What are you doing? I'm going to talk to her . . . but what's a Muslim girl doing talking so freely to me in the first place? I hope she doesn't think I'm hitting on her.*

We went to our seats, and I plunged right in. "Hey, listen," I said, "I gotta tell you something."

"What?" she asked, looking alarmed.

"If I tell you, you'll flip out and leave."

"You're freaking me out already. What are you talking about?"

"Okay, here it is. I am not a Muslim. I am married. I'm actually a Christian pastor." I told her all about my mom's dilemma and the reason for my trip. "I just can't be lying to you like this. You can go now, but I'd appreciate it if you wouldn't tell anybody about this."

"No, I'm not going to," she assured me. "I want to hear more."

So I told her everything, my story, the gospel. I ended it all by saying, "You know, I think God set this up for me to tell you about Jesus."

She told me she had always had a deep relationship with God. I said, as my flight was announced and I had to board, "If you want to get closer to God, the next step for you is Jesus."

We went our separate ways, and I have had no contact with her since. I may never know if she made a final decision to seek and follow Jesus. But then again she may be reading this today as a Christian.

Naeem Sahib

Pakistan is a shock to the system. Suffering in first-world countries like the United States or Kuwait tends to be more private, glossed over with affluence and technology and upward mobility, but in Pakistan, you can't avoid it. It is everywhere.

According to one study, the number of "absolute poor" in Pakistan is roughly 42 million. There is 62 percent of the population that cannot read, 61 million people have no access to safe drinking water, 54 million cannot get basic health services, and 9 million children under the age of five are malnourished.[1] Poverty-driven suicides are on an alarming uptick. No wonder some have referred to the situation in Pakistan as a "poverty bomb."[2]

Seen firsthand and in real time, these numbers are even more disturbing. The slums of Pakistan are basically omnipresent. When I was a kid on my only other visit to Lahore, I remember seeing a naked child playing in the gutter. As we rode past him in our rickshaw, I noticed that he was hunting for treasure in the filth at the side of the road. For a split second, our eyes met, and I remember thinking, *I never want to be that kid.* It was a defining moment, one that set the course of my early ambitions toward a life of relative affluence.

Even in the modest homes of Pakistan, there are servants. Everywhere, especially in the private homes, the caste system is clear. You bow or nod differently to a servant than you would to a peer or a superior. Mom stayed in her sister's home where there were servants who cooked, cleaned, and took care of the house. I couldn't get used to being called Naeem Sahib every time I turned around. *Sahib* means "master" in both Arabic and Urdu. Well, maybe I could get used to it if I had to. I once mentioned to Ashley how great it would be if she and the kids addressed me as *Sahib* or Master, but she wasn't too keen on the idea. I failed to get any buy-in from the kids either.

One of the first nights I was there, I was still feeling the effects of jet lag and couldn't sleep, so I walked out into the little courtyard of my aunt's house. I noticed one of the manservants lying on a narrow, wooden cot outside. He was awake, so I spoke to him. He sat up and answered, and we started a conversation. Before long, I grew tired of standing, so I sat down at the foot of his bed near his feet. He hopped up and all but shouted, "No, Naeem Saab, *aap yahaan nahi bet sak tae* (you cannot sit there)!"

He startled me, so I stood up too. "Why not?" I said. "Where *can* I sit?"

"Here, here," he patted the head of the bed, and I wondered if he was going to lie back down with his head on my lap. I almost told him I liked him, but not *that* much, but I had a feeling he wouldn't get the joke. He said, "You don't sit at my feet; I sit at your feet," as he sat down on the floor at my feet.

I said, "Nobody's sitting at my feet."

So we both stood up. Our conversation continued, but it was really awkward after that. I know some form of caste system exists in every culture, even in subtle ways in the United States, but it was unnerving in Pakistan where people are ranked by an arbitrary and unjust value system. It's a system that has taught people to limit themselves, to focus only on who they are and never on who they could be.

It was an interesting trip, that's for sure. A few days later relatives took me to visit the family of a potential bride they thought might interest me, because—remember—I was supposed to be single. This was a formal meeting, and I never interacted with the woman they all thought would make such a good match for me, who happened to be a distant cousin. Don't worry, it wasn't a date, but I was still tempted to blow my cover and tell them all about Ashley. Where was my wedding ring when I needed it?

BUSTED

My cousin, Mom's nephew, came to visit. He was the cousin I stayed with in Miami, the one who took me to the bus station for my trip to South Carolina when I first got to the States. My mom had helped to raise him, to pay for his education, and had recently loaned him a good bit of money when she lived in the States. She'd worked odd jobs while living in Charleston and had saved all her income, and she was very generous toward her extended family with it. At one point in her first year in Pakistan, when I imagine she grew weary of having no one to confide in, she revealed to this nephew that every one of her kids, his cousins, were Christians. She swore him to secrecy, and he agreed to keep a lid on the news.

One day when I was there, he said, grinning mysteriously, "Naeem, come get in the car. I want to take you somewhere special." Then he added this enigmatic caveat: "But you can't tell your mom."

I wasn't sure I wanted to go to this secret location with him. Against my better judgment, I got in the car and we took off. I plied him with questions, but he'd just look at me and say, "Just wait, you'll see."

During the drive he made a few veiled comments that led me to believe he must know more about me than he let on. Mom hadn't told me she had spilled our secret to him, but by the time we drove up to a house on the other side of the city, I put it all together. Knowing he knew made me nervous, especially when he looked sideways at me and said with a knowing smile, "Naeem, I know who you are."

But my fears were unfounded, at least for the time being.

We parked in a neighborhood and went into the home of an elderly Pakistani woman. Gathered there for lunch were a Catholic priest and a few other people. The woman told me, "I was your mom's neighbor when she was a young girl. I used to teach her all about Jesus."

Until this point, I'd assumed my mother had never heard about Jesus before, that her children were the first to tell her anything about him. But here in Pakistan was evidence that God had been pursuing my mom since before I was born. Just like Hagar, who when she was banished to the backside of a desert called him "a God of seeing" (Gen. 16:13), I was reminded that God sees us wherever we are. In the middle of Mom's hopeless situation, I found hope that God was chasing after her heart, just as he chased after mine.

BLACKMAIL

I left Pakistan without making any headway in my mom's case. The red tape there is even more convoluted and confusing than it is here, and I didn't get very far in my efforts to untangle it. Not long after I returned to the United States, Mom asked my cousin if he would pay her back what she had loaned him. Unlike in the States, Mom did not work in Pakistan. Not only did my cousin tell her no, he said that if she continued to demand that he return the money, he would tell everyone her secret. She said, partly out of irritation with this attempt at blackmail and partly out of a genuine need for cash, "Go ahead. Tell."

And so my cousin ratted her out. Now, in everyone's eyes,

my mom was a liar, nothing but a big sham. Her kids were all Christians, and her son had passed himself off as a single businessman when he was really a pastor of a Christian church, all with her apparent blessing. After that, whatever she said, no one would believe her. How could they? Mom's sister kicked her out of her house. This turn of events opened up a slew of new quandaries for my mom. Should she get a job? Could she get a job? Rent a place of her own? Settle down for the long haul? She had been in Pakistan two years by this point, and it looked as though she would be there a lot longer. In many ways she was at the mercy of her Pakistani family. And they were fiercely divided over what to do with her. Her brothers were all on her side. In fact, one of them came and picked her up from her sister's house and took her home. He offered to let her stay with him as long as she needed to. Her sisters, on the other hand, were venomous in their criticism of her. They cut her off completely.

Back home, we wondered if we'd ever see Mom again. The wait had reached excruciating proportions, and we were helpless to do anything to change her situation. In her absence, we had given her grandchildren she'd never met and celebrated family milestones without her. It felt like a death.

And then one day, Mom called me from Lahore. She had gotten a letter in the mail, and it looked like an approval for her American visa. By this time, my default mode was to presume the worst. "It's probably a mistake, Mom. Or a scam."

I didn't have the heart to tell her she might not have read it correctly. But she verified it there, and then we verified it here. God saw all along.

And then Mom came home.

ELEVEN

GROWING UP AND GETTING READY

When You said, "Seek My face," my heart said to
You, "Your face, O LORD, do I shall seek."

—PSALM 27:8, NASB

These days I don't mind sharing my church history. I am not ashamed to describe my first years as a follower of Jesus. Maybe a little embarrassed, but who doesn't wish for a replay of some of the foolish things they said and did when their zeal got the best of them? When I first arrived at Seacoast, I was still a brash believer in just about anything the televangelists had to sell. I named it and claimed it like a pro. I confess that more than once I "placed the affected area" of my body on the screen so a faith healer could pray for me. Yes, some people really do that.

You know how a newborn infant howls at birth, filling his or her lungs with air for the first time? It's not a very pretty sound, except maybe to his or her sentimental parents. Those first sounds are a little unsettling. That was me at first. I was a newborn with thirsty lungs, just doing my best to fill them up with the brand-new air of the Spirit. And if I thrashed around a little and made some noise in the process, well, that was just part of growing up.

One aspect of my immaturity was an unfocused, unbridled confidence. I thought this was a good quality. Until I learned better, I was more confident in what I could do for God than in what he could do for me. Remember how I told the senior pastor at Seacoast, Greg Surratt, that I would be on staff before long? I *told* him, not asked him or mentioned the possibility to him. I guess you could say I tried to name it and claim it with Pastor Greg, and it didn't work all that well.

Keep that conversation in mind as I fast-forward and share how my first full-time staff position at Seacoast, several years later, came about. I was making strides toward maturity, but I wasn't there yet. I had grown from a spiritual baby to an adolescent.

The two of us, Greg Surratt and I, were in the bathroom, and let's just say we weren't fixing our hair. He looked over and said to me, "Naeem, we're looking for a middle school director here. You interested?"

I didn't like the sound of that at all. I had just completed an internship at Seacoast, and now, while I did want to be on staff, I thought I was ready to be a "real" pastor. Maybe college or something a little more respectable. But seventh and eighth graders? No chance. Besides, I had no affinity with middle schoolers. Neither did I possess any of the skills or training necessary for the job.

"I don't know," I said, "I don't really have a heart for that."

"Why don't you pray for a heart for it," Greg said, "because right now that's what we got."

I went home, talked with Ashley, and I prayed about it just as Greg suggested. Then I went back to Greg and told him I was onboard. He told me something I agree with heartily now: if you can speak to a youth audience and grab their attention, you can speak to anybody. At that time I had absolutely no aspirations to be a senior pastor, but I had discovered I had a passion and a gift for speaking. I slowly began to develop another element in my growing character: fierce loyalty to my leaders combined with absolute trust in God. It wasn't long before Greg knew that if he asked me to do something, there would be no doubt; I'd do it. Of course, that meant if I failed in the process, it would be Greg's fault. I was finally gaining—in a twisted sort of way—a little healthy humility.

JV NITRO AND BEYOND

It wasn't a walk in the park. Nine kids showed up for the first Monday night meeting. It was pitiful. I decided to pour every ounce of crazy creativity I had into it. We switched the meeting to Wednesday nights, and, despite the pathetic beginning, it grew quickly. By the time we reached sixty to seventy kids, we got an old trailer and painted it. We called the group JV Nitro. I don't know about the kids, but I thought it was a cool name. That year we took a hundred and twenty teenagers to the Acquire the Fire conference. I have to admit, within a few months I had developed a heart for these kids. And I was having a boatload of fun in the process.

Meanwhile, six months into this gig, I was asked to take on the college ministry as well. Next I began to fill in with the high school ministry. The learning curve was steep, but I caught on eventually—that is, if catching on means figuring things out by making a *lot* of mistakes. But I got great hands-on training in leadership. I learned how to speak to groups. And I learned the value of mentors. I continued to meet with Michael Morris, but I sought out other youth leaders, too, like Joey Rumble, my first youth mentor. He was a lifesaver.

I really should issue a formal thanks to Seacoast and to Greg for hiring me in the first place. I wonder if they talked among themselves at a staff meeting, graciously of course, about what a gamble it would be to take me on. I had virtually no training. I still butchered the English language from time to time. I had zero experience with almost every cultural norm that contributed to the psyches of these thirteen- and fourteen-year-olds. The first retreat I took them on was a ski trip, and I had only seen snow once, and even then it was no more than a dusting in the flatlands of Charleston. I was a square peg for sure, but they took the risk that I might just make an interesting fit in a round hole, and I'm thankful they did.

I was still getting my feet wet in youth ministry when Greg approached me with another opportunity. The church had outgrown its facility, and one option they had explored was something everyone thought was a little nuts. He said he wanted to try something new: a satellite location. This was before *multisite* was a household word in evangelical church circles. "What do you think, Naeem?" he asked. "No one else thinks it's gonna work. Do you want to take a shot at it?"

Of course I did. Even when Greg joked that if it was a flop they'd have me deported. (They can't do that, can they?) I continued to oversee the college, high school, and middle school ministries at Seacoast. I had interns and staff who worked with me over a huge department that included some youth and all the young adults. I began to develop a launch team of young adults and college students in preparation for the service at our new location. Pastor Greg's two sons, Josh and Jason, were on this team. Before long we launched what we called the Annex at a strip-mall location that Easter. I may not have mentioned that I was an art major in college, so I had a blast designing the interior of our new meeting space. A local news article called it "The God Bar," so I assume that means the final product was pretty sweet. At first the Annex was mostly populated with singles and young adults, but pretty soon families started coming and bringing their children. It got more complicated to lead, so I gave up my ministry to youth and became the young adults' pastor.

I got involved in the creative team at Seacoast, teaching, writing, and contributing my two cents to planning our worship services. I had come a long way. I remember the first time they let me make announcements at a service. I felt pretty good about how I did on my first outing, until Greg came up after me and corrected almost everything I'd just said. It was funny later, but in my nervousness, I think I might have mixed up the details and invited middle school kids to a Celebrate Recovery meeting and instead of addressing college students, I said "anyone interested in college students." They even let me preach, and I thought I'd be clever and use one of Greg's pet idioms to describe an argument between Ashley and me. I meant to say we had "intense fellowship," but I got the phrase wrong and said we had "intimate fellowship." Apparently I said it—*wrong*—a number of times. Think about it. This was a crowd of predominately singles who thought they knew what I was talking about, but couldn't look one another in the eye when the subject was sex. Awkward. I wondered why people were on the edges of their seats. No telling what they thought I was going to say next, and they sure didn't want to miss it.

Keep Coming

During this time, we also began a Tuesday night gathering geared toward young adults. We called it Every Tuesday. In case you haven't noticed, despite the fact that English isn't my first language, I love a catchy title. We visited Louie Giglio's weekly event, called 722, in Atlanta and asked him to pray over us before we started. We decided to use one of my favorite verses in the Psalms as our foundation: "You have said, 'Seek my face.' My heart says to you, 'Your face, LORD, do I seek'" (Ps. 27:8).

The first night we planned for about fifty people to show up, and we were shocked when a hundred and thirty came. It was a huge rush for me to participate in something that I'd designed from the ground up. And it was clear that God was at work.

One Tuesday night, after I'd spoken to the group, a girl came up to me and said, "I have a friend who is a Muslim from Morocco."

She went on to describe this friend, and I could tell she was special to her. "You should invite her," I said.

"She's right here, behind me," and, as she said it, a girl stepped from behind her and introduced herself. It was a little awkward, but I introduced myself and asked, "So, what did you think about tonight? Your friend tells me you're Muslim."

"Yeah, I am," she said, "and I don't know what I think."

She had just arrived in Charleston and planned to attend college on a student visa. Although she'd grown up in Morocco and her parents were still there, she looked very Western, and I wondered how her parents felt about that. I responded with something like, "Well, that's cool. We'd love to see you again."

She seemed to appreciate how casual things were and the fact that there was no pressure. I talked to her that night about what it's like to be an international student and how important it was to make friends while she was here. Before the night was over, her friend approached me one more time, and I could tell she needed to talk.

"What do I do?" she asked. "How can I witness to her?"

"The fact that she's even here at a Christian church is crazy enough," I told her, "so I wouldn't force anything on her. Just keep asking her to come back, keep inviting her. Whatever you do, make sure she keeps coming."

By this time I had learned something important about the church. The presence of Jesus in a crowd of people who worship and love him is a powerful thing, mightier than the words we say. I think if we want to see God move in the hearts and lives of our friends, it helps to remember that context is often more powerful than content. This is coming from a preacher, from someone who's supposed to be all about content. But I've seen the gathered body of Christ do miracles in people's hearts too many times not to know it's true.

Her friend kept inviting her, and she kept coming. I would catch a glimpse of her in the crowd every Tuesday night for the next couple of months. And then one night after my sermon she came up to me, obviously crying. "I don't know what's going on," she said through her tears. "I feel like Jesus is drawing me. I think maybe this is true, but I just don't know."

I told her that sometimes our hearts respond to Jesus before our brains have a chance to catch up. That was certainly my story. That night she surrendered her heart and prayed to receive Christ. After that, no one had to invite her. She kept coming, week after week, for the next two years.

The last time I saw her, we met in a coffee shop after she'd called saying she needed to talk. She was about to graduate and go home to Morocco, and she wanted to know how to tell her Muslim parents about Jesus. She wondered how to approach things with them, knowing that they suspected some kind of change in her already. I told her not to lie, but to proceed with caution. I advised her from the Scriptures to be as wise as a serpent and as innocent as a dove (Matt. 10:16). And I reminded her of her own story. She agreed that the best kind of conversion is Holy Spirit led, not human engineered. I think that took the pressure off of her and gave her hope for her family. I'd like to give a glowing follow-up account here, but I don't have one. After she left the United States, we lost touch. This was before worldwide communication had become what it is today with e-mail and Facebook. But I believe, wherever she is, she is a bright light to the people around her.

VISION

I can't stress enough how much fun all this was. I felt I was in my sweet spot, and Ashley felt the same. We loved Charleston and Seacoast. If it wasn't so cheesy, we'd have worn matching "Life is Good" T-shirts every day and meant it. I wasn't looking to leave; in fact, all my daydreams about the future took place right there in Charleston at Seacoast.

What about my original dream of going as a missionary to India or some other country? I had not forgotten it, but in the absence of clear leading from Jesus and in the presence of so much satisfying work in Charleston, I had moved it to the back burner, and I didn't give it much thought. How could I, when there was so much going on at home?

During this time I went to hear Erwin McManus speak at a conference in Atlanta, and what he had to say just blew me away. I think God used Erwin to unsettle me enough to consider uprooting if that's what it took to fully engage in God's plan. He wrote in his book *Chasing Daylight*:

> The God of light insists on traveling into dark places; the God of peace continuously involves Himself in the wars of men; the God who is good engages the depth of human evil . . . To follow Jesus is to enter the unknown, to relinquish security, and to exchange certainty for confidence in Him.[1]

I was challenged by Erwin's words and by the daring way he was living them out in the diverse, multisite Mosaic Church in California. Erwin didn't necessarily plant discontentment with Seacoast in me, but he was the first to suggest that the vision God gave me might flourish more fully in a different setting. He also wrote, "You cannot follow God in neutral," and I agree.[2] Ashley and I were definitely not in neutral at Seacoast, but we were soon to discover another gear—one that would move us down a road we could never have imagined.

About that vision. One night as I stood in the crowd at the Every Tuesday service, minding my own business, God gave me a picture in my head, and it looked nothing like the here-and-now at Seacoast. I scanned the crowd, and for the first time I noticed something. We all—well, except for me—looked the same. Nearly everyone there was white. The vision God birthed in me that night looked completely different from my present setting.

I saw people from a multitude of cultures and backgrounds worshipping together. It was a small window into the future, but the image evoked a colorful mosaic that stunned me with its beauty and potential. I didn't have the name Mosaic yet in my mind, and I certainly didn't have the words *church planting* in my vocabulary. It wasn't until later that Erwin articulated what I saw in my vision and lent us the name for the church we would plant in Charlotte. But I look back on that night as the genesis of Mosaic Church. Sometimes God moves that way, stealthily, starting with the kernel of an idea. It may just be a glimpse, but it's a dramatic one, like the way the trees in your front yard light up for a brief nanosecond when lightning strikes.

Knowing how content Ashley and I were at the time, I wonder how I would have reacted if God had shown me the complete plan all at once. I'm pretty sure I would have balked.

To be honest, I did balk in small ways many times along the way. But in that moment I was stunned by this picture—this vision—of something that took my breath away with its beauty.

A CASE FOR DIVERSITY

For a long time I had sensed the personal implications of Jeremiah 1:5: "Before I formed you in the womb I knew you, before you were born I set you apart; I appointed you as a prophet to the nations" (NIV). Of course Ashley and I had discussed what this verse meant to us many times, both generally and specifically. While I loved every minute at Seacoast, I still had in the back of my mind the notion that someday God might up and send us to some uttermost nation. India, the country to which I thought I would go to do my faith-healing ministry, was not out of the question. But what was I to do with the way we seemed to fit here in the United States? Were we getting too settled, or was God simply preparing us for our unique calling to stay here in this country? The night God gave me the initial vision of Mosaic, I began to see that instead of sending me to the nations, God might bring the nations to me.

Here's the thing: God's heart has always been for the nations. From his covenant with Abraham, when he promised that, "in you all the families of the earth shall be blessed," (Gen. 12:3) to King David's claim that God would ultimately be "exalted among the nations" (Ps. 46:10), it is clear that God's blessings were never meant to be hoarded. My particular vision was nothing new. It had the heart of God and the history of the church behind it. The problem is that we humans lean toward sameness and security. We like to stay put. But from the beginning God's heart has been for us to, as he told Adam and Eve, "Be fruitful and multiply and fill the earth" (Gen. 1:28). He reiterated this command almost verbatim—twice—to Noah in Genesis 9. But again, humanity seems to crave a security that is rooted in the earth instead of in God alone. In Genesis 11, the people God created decided they'd better hedge their bets and maintain their sameness however they possibly could:

> And they said to one another, "Come, let us make bricks, and burn them thoroughly." And they had brick for stone, and bitumen for mortar. Then they said, "Come, let us build ourselves a city and a tower with its top in the heavens, and let us make a name for ourselves, lest we be dispersed over the face of the whole earth." (Gen. 11:3–4)

God's plan—to disperse the people he created in order to bless the earth—wasn't good enough for them. They decided to put down roots and avoid it at all cost. But God's purposes can't be thwarted by man's plans. He wanted them to scatter, so he confused their language in order to make it happen: "And from there the Lord dispersed them over the face of all the earth" (Gen. 11:9).

Then, in Genesis 12, God set in motion the genealogy that would one day birth a Redeemer for the entire human race. He chose Abraham and, through him and his descendants, promised that "in you all the families of the earth shall be blessed" (Gen. 12:3). God has never forgotten his desire to multiply his blessings to all nations.

One of the clear themes in my own story is the fact that God pursued me. This is an intensely personal fact, and, as these early verses in Scripture point out, a universal one as well. God's heart is set on pursuing us—people from every nation on earth. It always has been and always will be. And he will use whatever is necessary to seek and find us.

The church was founded on this same truth. Acts 8:1 describes a "great persecution," led by the apostle Paul (then known as Saul) that resulted in what Jesus commanded the disciples to do in the first place:

> And Saul approved of his execution. And there arose on that day a great persecution against the church in Jerusalem, and they were all scattered throughout the regions of Judea and Samaria, except the apostles.

This is how the Holy Spirit works, engineering circumstances for his will, pushing the church out to the nations. The early church fathers did not disperse with their heads down. They went out with a purpose: "Now those who were scattered went about preaching the word" (Acts 8:4). Philip went to the urban center of Samaria, and the ultimate result of his ministry there was "much joy in that city" (v. 8). Not much later, an angel appeared to Philip and directed him to "Rise and go toward the south to the road that goes down from Jerusalem to Gaza" (v. 26). I don't think it's a mistake that the scripture includes the small detail that this was a desert road. This wasn't a mission trip to a beach resort. It's also no mistake that God sent him to a particular man. This man was "an Ethiopian"—a man of color, from a different race (v. 27). From a country that, in those days, was considered the uttermost reaches of the known, civilized world.

"A eunuch"—a man of a different, indeterminate sexual identity.

"A court official of Candace, queen of the Ethiopians"— an influential man.

A man who was "in charge of all her treasure"—a wealthy man (v. 27).

Philip was a minor player in this drama. The way I see it, the Holy Spirit was the focal point, the one who directed the entire encounter from start to finish. It could not be clearer that God's heart is for all people, and that he will dispatch us to the far corners of the earth to make sure everyone knows it. This story is a microcosm of the vision I had for Mosaic. Ashley and I began to dream of a place for people like the Ethiopian.

People who are different colors.

People who are from different nations.

People who are broken and confused in their sexuality.

People whose lives can be influenced by the gospel and who can, in turn, influence others.

People who, whether they are poor or affluent or somewhere in between, can get their deepest needs met and learn to meet the needs of others.

The end goal of this vision isn't numbers or programs or buildings. It is joy. Because joy is God's response when the nations are reached, when a person who is lost is found: "Just so, I tell you, there will be more joy in heaven over one sinner who repents than over ninety-nine righteous persons who need no repentance" (Luke 15:7).

We knew that this vision, however it unfolded, would never

be about us. It would ultimately be about men and women reflecting the glory of God. And we prayed it would result in these same men and women doing exactly what the Ethiopian did when Philip disappeared. He "went on his way rejoicing" (Acts 8:39).

TWELVE

MOSAIC

How in the world could you ever imagine a life of faith that does not require risk? Faith and risk are inseparable.

—ERWIN MCMANUS

IF A VISION IS FROM God, there will be that moment when it seems downright ridiculous. Scratch that; it *will* be downright ridiculous. Even so I believe God is continually about the business of speaking to us, and by now I hope I've made a case for listening for his voice, even if it comes to you in a whisper and even if that whisper sounds a little strange. Or very strange.

Just look at the vision God gave Moses. Compared to anything in my experience and probably in yours, too, Moses' story is beyond strange. Moses, who was by all accounts running away from his life and his responsibilities, saw a burning bush in the desert and had a conversation with it, or rather with God who was in the bush. Now if that doesn't seem bizarre enough for you, what God asked Moses to do was just about as insane as the fact that such a conversation ever happened in the first place. God told Moses to go back to Egypt and plead with Pharaoh to let his people go.

This was the same Pharaoh who was the most powerful man in the civilized world, who had armies and sorcerers at his beck and call, who owned most if not all of Egypt's gross national product. Imagine strolling into the Oval Office to deliver a personal message to the president, and you get the idea. This is the same Pharaoh who would most likely have considered Moses a pathetic poser, a slave who had had the gall to pass himself off as royalty. It was the same Pharaoh who, by law, would probably arrest Moses and slam his sorry backside in jail if he showed up back in Egypt. Now there on the backside of the desert where he had a family, a job, and relative security, God interrupted Moses' life to send him on this harebrained errand.

Spoiler alert: Moses eventually did it, and Pharaoh eventually let his people go, but not without a lot of drama in the meantime. A portion of the drama was due to the fact that Moses is just like us. When faced with a clear vision from God—which, of course, sounded insane—he had a few issues on his way to faith and obedience. Because I'm keenly aware of these issues, having dealt with them on numerous occasions myself, I've listed them for you here. When God gives us a vision, we typically respond in a certain way:

1. FIRST, we think it won't work. We're like, "God I know you've been thinking about this for longer than me, and I love your idea, I really do, but let me tell you something. I'm intuitive, and I process well, and I've been thinking, too, and I've come to a different conclusion. It just won't work, God."

We proceed to enumerate the many reasons God's plan is

a bad idea. To God. As if he hasn't considered the worst-case scenario as thoroughly as we have. That's what Moses did at first. Right off the bat he anticipated problems with God's big idea and told him all about those problems. He knew the people would ask questions about this burning-bush God, and he wondered, "If I come to the people of Israel and say to them, 'The God of your fathers has sent me to you,' and they ask me, 'What is his name?' what shall I say to them?" (Ex. 3:13). God answered that he was the I AM of Abraham, Isaac, and Jacob. But Moses still had his doubts: "But behold, they will not believe me or listen to my voice, for they will say, 'The LORD did not appear to you'" (Ex. 4:1).

Maybe if Moses had paid closer attention, he would have understood that "How?" is never the right question when faced with an impossible vision, especially one delivered from a burning bush. I know, I know. I wouldn't have done any better. But the right question about a vision from God is not how; it's why. God doesn't issue random, purposeless visions. He always has a motive. The reason for the vision God gave Moses is clear: "I have surely seen the affliction of my people who are in Egypt and have heard their cry" (Ex. 3:7). I suspect this is the same motivation for many of the dreams God instills in his people today. God still hears the cries of the hurting, the lost, and the dying. The visions he gives to us are anchored in this same "why." And the "why" is always anchored in his heart.

2. SECOND, we assume we don't have the proper or adequate skills to do what God has asked us to do. We presume that it's all on us and that we can't do it. We think we have to carry the whole thing with our own resources, our talents, and

our skills. It's interesting that this argument is the one thing that ticked God off during his conversation with Moses in the desert. Perhaps this was because what God *knew*—that Moses was not limited by his own gifts and resources—was diametrically opposed to what Moses *believed*. God explained to him that Aaron was on the way, in the wings and ready to be on his team. He had resources at the ready, even though Moses couldn't see them yet.

A pastor friend of mine once said, "I can do anything," and I couldn't help but doubt him. Wouldn't you? It sounded kind of arrogant to me. He stubbornly asserted it again: "I can do anything. Any of the complicated stuff out there. I can build a bridge, launch a booster rocket, write a textbook, teach quantum physics, tie the stem of a cherry into a knot in my mouth [well, maybe he didn't mention that last one]. Just give me the right team." It sounds a little cocky, but it's true. Resources are not an issue with God. If he asks us to do something, he'll show up with the resources to handle it.

Remember the movie *Apollo 13*? During one of the many tense moments in the film, a group of earthbound engineers must figure out a way to fix the carbon dioxide converter on the *Apollo 13* out in space so the astronauts will have enough oxygen to make it home alive. They've got to make a plan and then walk the astronauts through it. A guy dumps the contents of a cardboard box onto a table and tells the huddle of other nerdy guys to get to it. This pile of stuff mostly looks like junk, but it represents exactly what the *Apollo 13* astronauts, James Lovell, Jack Swigert, and Fred Haise, had onboard at their disposal, and nothing more. If you haven't seen the movie, you probably still know the outcome. They made a carbon dioxide converter out of unlikely materials, including duct tape and cardboard, and the astronauts made it home still breathing. It's a great story, but it pales in comparison to what God can do. *His* cardboard box is never empty. And his creative ingenuity is boundless.

3. THIRD, when the vision God gives us is more daunting than we can handle—and again, it should be—we tell him to send someone else. "I appreciate the honor, God," we say, "but I think you've got the wrong guy. I don't have a problem with your idea. Go for it, but send someone else. It's okay by me if you burn a big, ole tree instead of a bush for the next guy, but I think I should pass on this one. I'll pray for that guy. I'll even write a support check. But this isn't me."

Have you ever seen something mildly dangerous or embarrassing happen in public, like a pratfall on the sidewalk or a spilled drink in a restaurant, and your immediate reaction is to think, *Somebody oughta take care of that?* You acknowledge the necessity of action, but you're content to be nothing more than a spectator. We're all prone to idling in bystander status. But if the vision is from God and if it is tied to his heart—his reason—then it's time to listen and act.

Hebrews 11 tells us what prompted Moses to finally respond to the vision God gave him and what kept him in the game over and over:

> By faith Moses, when he was grown up, refused to be called the son of Pharaoh's daughter, choosing rather to be mistreated with the people of God than to enjoy the fleeting pleasures of sin. He considered the reproach of Christ greater wealth than the treasures of Egypt, for he

was looking to the reward. By faith he left Egypt, not being
afraid of the anger of the king. (vv. 24–27)

It was faith. You may think, *Well, it was easy for Moses to
have faith. He had a burning bush, a staff that turned into a snake,
and all those other cool miracles to convince him.* But Hebrews
11 won't let us come to that conclusion so easily. Let me finish
Hebrews 11:27 for you: "he endured as seeing him who is invisible." Invisible! Now, that's crazy. But Moses was just like us.
God grew his faith as he locked eyes on him, the Invisible One.

Moses wasn't the only Old Testament person to have this
kind of faith. Hebrews 11 lists a bunch of big names, starting
with Abel and followed by an impressive list of men and women
who fixed their gazes on the Invisible One just as Moses did.
Most of the people on that list had very little empirical evidence to support their faith.

In spite of circumstances that looked even less promising
than Moses' did in the desert, Abram trusted "in the presence
of the God in whom he believed, who gives life to the dead and
calls into existence the things that do not exist" (Rom. 4:17).
Abram believed in the promise God gave him that he would
have a son, even when he was nearing a hundred years old, and
it certainly looked as if God was never going to make good on
that promise. Keeping his eyes on the Invisible Promise Giver
grew Abram into a faith giant:

No unbelief made him waver concerning the promise of
God, but he grew strong in his faith as he gave glory to God,
fully convinced that God was able to do what he had promised. (vv. 20–21)

And that's the only way our faith can grow too. As I share some of the ups and downs of Mosaic, from the first days until now, know that the Invisible One went before us and behind us, whether we could see him at the time or not. Through it all, Ashley and I have learned to trust God more and more by locking our eyes on him. We want to be like Moses, who "had his eye on the One no one can see, and kept right on going" (Heb. 11:27 MSG).

Just a few weeks ago I got a call from the parents of a young man who came to faith here at Mosaic but who had moved away from Charlotte. His father told me their son had died in a freak accident just days before, and he wanted to know if I would speak at his funeral. As always, death puts life in perspective. With full confidence, I was able to look in the eyes of those grieving parents and say, "This good-bye that is breaking your hearts is not forever. This is merely 'See you later.' There is more to this life, much more. There is an unconquerable life afterward."

The young man's father said, "Thank you so much for what you did for our son." And this—one person's gratitude for something bigger than anything I or any one of us can do—reminded me that the Invisible One is as real as anything I can see with my eyes or touch with my fingers.

Time to Go

Fast-forward from the initial vision to a conversation I had with Erwin McManus a little while later. At some point in the process of the visual image becoming a decision, Erwin—a guy who I am certain sees the Invisible God—said to me, "You need to move to Charlotte to start a church called Mosaic."

This was not a new idea; it was simply a confirmation of the one that had been marinating and taking shape for some time. I won't bore you with the research and the many conversations that led to this point. From the beginning we knew Charleston was not the place to plant a culturally diverse church, not when other Southern cities reported some of the fastest-growing immigrant populations in the country. The demographics in Charlotte were far more varied than in genteel, white, traditional Charleston. Of the several cities we considered, it was also the closest to our families, just a day's drive away from Charleston or Greenville. As the largest city in North Carolina, it was also much more urban than Charleston. So we eventually settled on Charlotte, with its remarkable boom of multi-ethnic and multi-racial growth, as the most strategic city for a mosaic of worshippers to gather and create a community of believers. By the time Ashley and I agreed over breakfast to take steps toward church planting in another city, I was ready to break the news to Greg and the rest of the staff at Seacoast.

Greg was immediately supportive. Even more, he saw that God had moved us, and he said, "You need to do this."

But Greg is a realist too. I asked him, "Do you think it'll work?" You know, hoping for a verbal fist pump or a fatherly pat on the back or something like that.

He said, in that matter-of-fact way he has, "We'll see."

This was a subtle reminder that—in human terms—the odds were against me. No odds had been quantified yet, because as far as we could tell, no one like me—a Pakistani from Kuwait and an Arab-looking man—had attempted to plant a church in the post-9/11 South. Greg's response was, believe it or not, my first clue that this thing was going to be harder than I thought.

It took us six months to leave. Conversations—lots of them—turned into strategies and finally celebrations. By the time the last good-bye party took place, I imagine people wondered why we were still around. We shared our vision over and over. Greg had already told us to feel free to recruit people. "Take whoever you want," he said. We didn't exactly ask anyone in particular to join us in the move to Charlotte; we just shared the vision and our passion to make it happen. When the time came to go, we had a team of about thirty people, mostly singles and young, married couples, who decided to relocate with us.

We teamed up with Mosaic in Los Angeles, with the ARC church-planting network (the Association of Related Churches), and, of course, with Seacoast. One thing I've observed about church planting today is that it works best when approached synergistically. One guy forging into new territory all alone with only his immediate family for support is a bad model, and one that is doomed to fail. I'm grateful for the many people who joined us; some offered support and wisdom from afar and others stood shoulder to shoulder with us in the trenches.

"I Pity da Fool"

As an eighties kid in Kuwait, I loved American TV shows, especially the fantastically macho ones like *The A-Team*. What kid of that era didn't secretly wish he could look and talk like Mr. T? But my real hero was the crusty, cigar-chomping mastermind behind the mischief in every episode, Hannibal. I still get a kick out of his patented phrase: "I love it when a plan comes together."

Because I do too. A plan that truly comes together with precision is a thing of beauty. But sometimes plans refuse to act like television, especially plans that are prompted by God's vision. They take twists and turns, and sometimes they even fail miserably. I've noticed that the stories of the Bible often play out smack dab in the middle of stressful, unsuccessful, even wretched moments. The biblical visionaries flirted with failure over and over. Moses led the Israelites through the Red Sea in triumph, but can you imagine what it was like the night before? The "strong east wind" that blew up and parted the waters probably just made matters worse at first (Ex. 14:21). I'm sure there were some naysayers who grumbled, "Isn't it enough that we have to be scared out of our wits by Pharaoh's army closing in on us? Have you noticed, they're getting closer? And now there's this blasted wind. My beard is blowing into my face."

Our plans for Mosaic started out great. We knew we'd need a killer worship leader if we were going to start strong, so we were delighted when a very talented, seasoned leader at Seacoast volunteered to be a part of our launch team. With this important detail securely buttoned up, we left for a family vacation—a cruise with Ashley's family—encouraged that things were well under way for our imminent move and the eventual launch of Mosaic. By then Asher was two, and we had decided our little family could manage this trip only if we could work out babysitting onboard the ship. Everything was set. Or so we thought.

The day we boarded the cruise ship, we discovered there

was no care offered for kids Asher's age after all, so we now had a two-year-old with us every moment of the trip. Not a big deal normally. But have you ever been on a cruise? With a toddler?

One morning early in our trip, we realized we hadn't seen Ashley's dad, so we went looking for him. When we found him in his room, he smiled at us . . . with only half of his face. We assumed he'd had a stroke. We got him off the boat and to an emergency room, where they stabilized him and discovered he had Bell's Palsy, which can mimic a stroke. But you can imagine the bedlam that ensued for the rest of the trip. Ashley's dad was not allowed back on the ship for the duration because of insurance liability issues, so he and her mom flew home before our trip was over. The next day Ashley's sister contracted food poisoning, so we made another emergency-room trip. Oh, and did I mention that I was basically blind in one eye for most of the week after I lost my contact lens in the pool on the first day? It was the vacation from hell. And I'm only telling you half of it.

I'm not sure if Murphy's Law exists, but what happened next makes me wonder. The ship docked, and we were never more relieved for a vacation to end. When our ride finally showed up at the port an hour after every other passenger had left, we were met with some news that made the hassles and hardships of the preceding days pale in comparison. The friend who picked us up said, "I guess you heard about (the worship leader who was going to join us in Charlotte)?"

No, we not very patiently explained to her. We had been aboard a ship and had not heard any news, local, national, or otherwise. "It was all over the papers," she said, not one to beat around the bush. "He's in jail."

Then she told us the whole story, and even though it's public record, I'd rather not repeat it here.

But that's not all. My mom's deportation to Pakistan happened the year before our move. The stress of never knowing if or when she'd be allowed back into the States assaulted us on a daily basis. The week before we moved to Charlotte I made my incognito trip to Pakistan. Not what I'd call good timing. A few months later, the week before the launch of our first Mosaic service in Charlotte, my dad suffered a heart attack in Charleston and had quadruple bypass surgery. Of course I spent the week before the launch in Charleston with my dad instead of in Charlotte dealing with the many details of the launch service. Dad is fine now, but it was a hard, touch-and-go week.

I share all this to point out that Mosaic was not born in a vacuum. You could say this is the story of my life, and I suspect the same theme plays out in yours as well. Out of the brokenness and the chaos of real life, God fashions something beautiful and redemptive. It took the Gulf War to push me from Kuwait to South Carolina. It took a full-on, evil attack by demons for me to recognize the powerful reality of Jesus. God used me, a new pastor who was also a husband, a dad, and a son, who had a life that refused to slow down and certainly wasn't stress free, to plant a church.

But amid all this mayhem, there was evidence of God's favor every step of the way. We met with a Charlotte restaurant owner right off the bat who gave us great insight into possible locations for the church—including a newly developed mall— that would strategically place us near the kinds of people we wanted to meet and reach. By the time we moved, we had a worship leader with us who was a very talented and charismatic guy. Another man who had amazing logistics training and gifts joined us. A man at Seacoast, a former CFO of a Fortune 500 company, approached me just before we moved and told me that he and some other men in the church had developed a team called Angels of Mosaic. The purpose of this group was to intervene with resources if at any time we got in a financial bind that first year. Until he told me, we had no idea they were even there, primed and ready to bless us.

BEGINNINGS

We were off and running. Our launch team started out as a young-adult small group of thirty people that met in our home every Sunday night. We visited churches all over Charlotte on Sunday mornings. Before long the launch team was too large for our living room, and we needed a new location. We moved to a neighborhood clubhouse but quickly outgrew that too. Once again, we were on the lookout for a bigger venue, one we hoped would serve us when we launched. Every single one of us was new to the area, so our networking capacity was severely limited, but God works outside our limitations. I wonder if he may even laugh at them.

Location turned out to be a big glitch for a reason I never expected. I forget what I look like sometimes. That can be an issue if you live in the South and look like me. I never considered Charlotte "the South." It's north of Charleston, after all. Anyway, we thought it would be a great idea to hold our meetings in a school, so we started hunting for the right one.

I remember a group of us walked into the very first school on our list to check it out. I'm assuming when they discovered that I—the Arab-looking guy—was the pastor of this church that wanted to use their building, they told us, "You have to leave. Now." They walked us to the parking lot and said, "You will never have a church here."

I was a little shocked by that, and I was even more surprised when it kept happening. Every single school closed their doors in our faces. Not too long ago, a woman confessed to me that she had pegged me for a member of a terrorist sleeper cell who was infiltrating the church, and it took her a long time to be convinced otherwise. Someone else told me I was "too Middle Eastern" to be trusted as his pastor. At another school, while we waited in the lobby, we overheard someone in the office say, "Don't you bring him in here." I talked to Greg about it, and he had a really pragmatic solution: "Send somebody else."

"Seriously?" I said.

"Seriously. I know you forget what you look like, buddy. And a name like Naeem doesn't help. And now that I think about it, Mosaic sounds a little like mosque, doesn't it?"

One day a guy showed up at our house to fix our garage door. Ashley was home, and this man sensed the Lord wanted him to talk with her. She told him why we had moved to Charlotte and a little about our plans for the future. He then told her about a warehouse we could use to store all our stuff. We found an AMC theater where we could meet. We ended up using it at no cost until our launch Sunday, and after that we paid a whopping two hundred dollars a month for it. As the day of our first service neared, we struck a verbal contract with the theater, but we didn't get it in writing until two weeks before the launch. Given our problems with finding a venue in the first place, that was really unnerving.

We'd moved to Charlotte in September, and before long we had about seventy people on our launch team. We started meeting on Sunday mornings. We prayed and fasted together. We became a community with a burning mission to reach Charlotte. We blitzed our part of the city with mailers and prayed over them as we posted them. We put signs in the bathrooms of local restaurants and gyms. Often while eating at a restaurant, the server would say, "I saw you in the women's bathroom." (My mug was on the signs.) We put decals on our cars. People were talking about Mosaic before it actually existed. I got to know the faith editor of the local paper, and he came to our launch service and wrote a glowing story that drew in more people.

The first Sunday, we had no idea how many people would show up. We had advertised gas giveaways, but would anyone show up for those? When 430 people showed up for the first service, we were shocked. We had to use overflow space that very first service. We quickly went to two services, and by Easter we had over 500 in attendance. The following Easter, just a few months after our first anniversary, more than one thousand people came to four services. By then we had added a Sunday night service geared toward young adults that met in a music venue downtown.

We were still run by a mostly volunteer staff. Ashley was pregnant with our daughter, Nurah, and, no doubt, relieved when we added the Sunday night service. Now the sixty young adults who had begun to show up at our house every Sunday night had somewhere else to go. I was having a ball, and Ashley was too, but even high-energy people have thresholds. We were wearing out, and we'd only just begun. Jason, a youth ministry guy who volunteered in Charlotte while running his business in Charleston, paid for my assistant that first year, but our growing church generated more work than one administrative person could do on her own, even one as talented and faithful as she was. To be honest, all of us were growing weary of the effort it took to stay afloat in this vast ocean of growth. Leadership fatigue probably played a part in what happened next, but—as is always the case—it was way more complicated than that.

Beginnings Have Their Share of Endings

My old nemesis, my Middle Eastern appearance, continued to cause a few interesting opportunities here and there. One family in the UK did a little research after their Muslim daughter came to faith and decided I was the culprit. They contacted me, and let's just say it wasn't nice. I got this shady, anonymous letter that included a picture of me from the paper and another photo of a terrorist attack. Nothing came of it, but it was enough to rattle us and to cause us to report it to the local police.

During our first few years, my biggest fear was that there would be another attack on American soil. To be honest, I still dread the fallout if that were to happen again. There would be people who would look at me and say, "Why the heck are we following this guy?" I just know it. But the color of my skin was definitely not our only problem, and it wasn't the reason for the near-demise of Mosaic after that first year.

Let me summarize year two of Mosaic: crash and burn. No, it wasn't fatal, but it was a hemorrhage. It's too fresh and, honestly, too personal for me to spell out the specifics in writing anytime soon. The generalities are bad enough. We bled people and leaders for several years after that. In fact, the healing process didn't begin until two or three years ago.

But these details are for another book.

Why even hint at this part of the story? For starters, it would be disingenuous to leave this chapter of our story out. It would seem as if I only wanted you to know the successes and none of the failures. I have a feeling most church planters, if they experience the high of rapid growth, at some point also experience the low of attrition. And it's painful. If you're a church planter, I hope this part of my story encourages you. I don't necessarily agree that "what doesn't kill you makes you stronger," but I do know that absolutely nothing Satan throws at us is fatal. Not only that, but the worst mess a church planter encounters can turn into a platform from which he or she can more powerfully proclaim God's power to heal and restore.

The God we do not see works behind the scenes in the messes we do see. But, like I said, that's for another book.

When I think about where the church is now and where I think, by God's grace, we're headed, I realize it's important to understand that we are an imperfect body. We, like every other church that has ever existed, have our share of war stories. But we also know the ultimate end of the story: our enemy is defeated and our King reigns eternal.

THIRTEEN

GOD OUT
OF CONTEXT

*It never failed to amaze me how the most ordinary
day could be catapulted into the extraordinary in the
blink of an eye.*

—JODI PICOULT

DESPITE MY UNIQUE ORIGINS AND the supernatural drama
of my conversion to Christ, I'm basically an ordinary guy, and
I suspect my days are no less ordinary than yours. Believe it or
not, I find that the ordinary stories in my life give me some of
the most bizarre windows into the extraordinary work of the
Holy Spirit. And the best sermon illustrations.

As I said, I'm ordinary. Ashley and I work out at the gym,
cook dinner together at home, drive our daughter to gymnas-
tics, and watch movies together. And in the middle of all this
average stuff, things happen.

Like the day when I was in Target, and I saw a woman who looked vaguely familiar. Charlotte is not a small town. Our population is bumping up against an impressive one million mark, but you can still have those unexpected moments when you run into people you know. The problem this time was that I could not for the life of me figure out who this woman was or how I knew her.

She and I looked at each other with identical expressions on our faces. You know, the one that says, *I know I know you. But how?* I began a rapid-fire countdown of places, neat categories where she might fit. The kids' school? Maybe. The gym? Maybe. Mosaic? Maybe. I was a little worried about that one because you'd think I would recognize people who go to the church I pastor. Or at least most of them. Some of them?

Before I finished my mental list, recognition dawned on her face, and she said, "Starbucks."

Yes, that was it! Erica, my Starbucks barista. Well, not "mine," but if you're like me you feel like you kind of own the place. The minute I realized who she was, I couldn't believe I had not recognized her before.

I'm not worried that my finely tuned memory is fading. At least not enough to send me to a neurologist. This lapse was understandable because Erica was outside of her normal context. If she'd been wearing a black apron and, better yet, if she'd handed me my coffee, I would have known her right away. Context is a powerful tool we all use to keep our lives and our memories organized. So powerful that it jars us when someone or something shows up in the wrong category—when they are out of context. That makes context a big deal.

The Lost Art of Noticing

Some of us are more aware of our contexts than others. Maybe that's you. You notice things, like your wife's new haircut, your husband's shaved chin after years of sporting a goatee, or the bold, new color painted on the house down the street. You are a noticer by nature. But many of us fall on the opposite end of the continuum between noticing and oblivion. We don't pick up on the present realities that play out day after day right under our noses. We don't sense the subtle shifts and cues going on around us. *Yeah, that's me,* you may be thinking. *I can't help it; most of the time I'm pretty oblivious.*

But sometimes noticing is absolutely necessary, whether we have the tendency for it or not. You don't think so? Ask yourself these questions: Do you notice the loneliness in the eyes of your cashier at the drugstore? Do you see the pain on your neighbor's face when you ask about her children? Do you pick up on the unspoken frustration in your child's eyes when he or she gets home from school? Do you see these things or do you miss them? This is why noticing is important. Noticing others is a love skill we need to develop, because nothing communicates love more powerfully than noticing.

Context can make noticing tricky. Life is full of out-of-context moments like that one I had in Target. But it's what God said to me on the way home that made me think about noticing in a different way.

Yes, God continues to speak to me. At times it has been strange, like that first night when he rescued me and told me my life was not my own. But, believe it or not, that was ordinary. Because God doesn't just speak to weird, Middle Eastern guys; he speaks to ordinary people. And he speaks to us in ordinary places, like in the car in the parking lot at Target.

Naeem, do you know what I look like out of context? You recognize me in the places you create for me, like worship services and Christian conferences, but do you see me anywhere else?

In the quiet of my car on the way home that day, I had to admit it was true. Sure, I recognize God in church, in my quiet devotional times, and in prayer gatherings and Bible study meetings. God is easy to spot in those contexts. But what about everywhere else? I talk as if God only exists in the places I have engineered for him.

What about you? We notice God's presence in certain people and we say others are far away from him. We say God is powerfully present in a particular place, and we call other places "godforsaken." We may call a coincidence "a God thing," while the rest of life is mundane. But what if there is no place, no context in which God does not exist? What if there is no situation, no pain, and no crisis where God is not at its center? What if God's DNA exists in each and every person? That would mean my encounter with Christ twenty years ago is not all that unique. It would also mean God wants to have life-altering interactions with us no matter our contexts. It might even mean he has already initiated the conversation. And although we may not notice God, we can be sure he notices us.

It would be all too easy to assume the highlight of my story happened in that moment in a dark room when Jesus noticed me; when he showed up to vanquish demons and, consequently, to rock my world; when he answered the nonchalant prayer of a cocky, young Muslim boy. I was out of context. At that time, everything about my context made God noticing me seem like an impossibility, not to mention my noticing him. Although I was not in Kuwait at the time, my culture and my identity was rooted in Islam. I was in the Bible Belt, but I didn't fit there. I was not a white American. I was young and ambitious, and decidedly not humble. Isn't humility the necessary condition for God to work in us? I was in a bedroom, not a church building or a meeting room full of Christians with their sermons and music and spiritual buzz. I am still in awe that God noticed me at all. As the psalmist says, "He drew me up from the pit of destruction, out of the miry bog" of my unlikely context (Ps. 40:2). But my story isn't complete if it stops there. Because God didn't stop there.

An Invisible Woman

The Bible is full of stories like mine, where God took note of people who were invisible, in everyone else's opinion. In a story recorded in Luke 8, Jesus noticed a woman who took not being noticed for granted. She was a widow, which meant she had no recognizable or legitimate identity in her culture. She had been sick for years on end, which probably meant her friends ignored her. Doctors had tried to help and finally gave up on her. Hopelessness was her middle name. She was so convinced of her own invisibility that when Jesus came to town, and a tiny spark of hope flickered inside her, she assumed he would not have time for her. But if she could just touch the hem of his robe, slip past, and grab a blessing from him without his knowledge, well, surely that was worth trying.

The hem on Jesus' robe was a bigger deal than any hem we

might imagine today. The Messiah was said to appear "with healing in his wings," and the Rabbis wore tassels on their hems to represent this prophecy (Mal. 4:2 NLT). The woman probably thought to herself, *I won't bother the guy. Everybody wants a piece of him. The hem is all I need, so I'll touch it and be gone.*

Her strategy should have worked. The passage says the crowd that surrounded Jesus "pressed around" him (Luke 8:42). We're not talking a few people mingling and chatting around him; we're talking a European-soccer-match-riot-ready-to-happen–sized crowd. The woman should have been fine just adding her fingerprint to Jesus' already-smudged clothing. But no. Jesus, it turns out, was a noticer of the first degree.

"Who was it that touched me?" Jesus asked (Luke 8:45).

After what was probably an awkward pause (because in a crowd like that, touching—appropriate and inappropriate—is as commonplace as a brushed elbow in a crowded elevator), Peter finally stated the obvious: "Master, this whole crowd is pressing up against you" (v. 45 NLT). Jesus asked the question not because he was finicky about his personal space, but because he noticed that the woman needed something specific from him and because that very thing had "gone out from" him to her (v. 46 NLT). An exchange occurred between the two of them that Jesus was not content to let slip his notice.

I know when we hear this story preached from a pulpit we're usually told that we play the role of the woman. We are the ones who can reach out and touch the hem of Jesus' garment. If Jesus noticed her, surely he will notice us.

It's not a bad application of the passage. Our stories always start with the truth that God notices us. Where would any of us be if he didn't? We only love him because he first loved us, right? But God intends for us to also notice *him*. The very purpose of the incarnation, the appearance of God here on earth in human form, was for the Creator of the universe to make himself known in our context. We know from Psalm 139 and plenty of other places in Scripture that God sees us before we're even born. And then he spends a lifetime getting us to see him. But, again, my story doesn't end there, and neither should yours.

What if there's more to the Luke 8 story? What if the disciples were meant to understand that while they could find healing in his touch, the ultimate role they were to play from that point on was not of the woman but of Jesus himself? And what if this is the crux of the story for us as well? We're supposed to be Jesus. That's who we are, after all. Ever since Paul stood before Agrippa, the world has called us Christians, or "little Christs" (Acts 26:28).

Being Jesus means noticing people just as Jesus noticed the woman. While that may not sound like a big deal, it is. Colossians 1:15 beautifully illustrates this complex mystery. The apostle Paul referred to Jesus as "the visible image of the invisible God" (NLT). This word *image* is *eikon* in Greek, the word from which we get our word *icon*. At the risk of modernizing an ancient idea a little too much, consider how we use the word today. If you tap or click an icon on your computer or mobile device, an entire world unfolds before your eyes—one that the icon indicated would be there, just a click away.

From the beginning of time, God has used images to showcase himself to the world, to hint that he is speaking and moving in our midst. He was on display in the Old Testament in the parting of the Red Sea, in the provision of manna and water in the desert, and in the words of Moses and the prophets. From Genesis to Malachi, men and women gave witness that God was present and involved. And then came the clearest *eikon* of all: Jesus. By his birth, life, death, burial, and resurrection, Jesus kept the conversation between the Father and his creation alive. He left behind the Holy Spirit to comfort us with his presence and to compel us to represent him to others.

Being Jesus to the world means being the visible representation of the invisible God to people who think they themselves are invisible. It means noticing them, and thereby reminding them that they are not.

Who are these invisible people? I don't think I need to tell you. You know. They are the people who get lost in the crowd. Who are forgotten in our busyness. Who seem to live their lives on mute, whether it's because they lack confidence or have experienced too much hurt to live out loud. Invisible people are the people who serve us—garbage collectors and cashiers and the waitstaff at our favorite restaurants. They are the ones who stand at the edge of the photograph and get cropped out, who sit on the back row so they can leave early, who by their quiet lives refuse to make a splash anywhere. The people who don't fit into our contexts.

Airport Sushi Is a Bad Idea, But . . .

Could it be that God is more at work outside the walls of our churches than he is inside them? I've decided to take a risk and assume that he is.

When I travel, I've begun noticing people more. Just a little attempt to be more like Jesus. I get kind of excited, wondering what God is going to do. Looking like I look, air travel can be an adventure, but that's not what I'm talking about. The art of noticing is an acquired skill. I've discovered that I may notice someone, but then I make quick assumptions about them, and those assumptions can be all wrong.

A few years ago I got on a small plane. You know, one of those where you hope the person next to you is skinny, and not a toddler. My seatmate looked like a white, wannabe rapper, gangsta bling, baggy pants, and all. He sat down and said a gruff, "Hey," and put his headphones on. So I said hey and put my headphones on.

The flight attendant came by and my hip-hop buddy ordered some alcohol. Suddenly, he got chatty. He was barely twenty, on leave from the military, and headed to see his fiancée. The fiancée was pregnant, which was why she'd been bumped from girlfriend status to fiancée. The more he talked, I detected a pretty thick European accent I couldn't place, so I asked him where he was from. Turns out he was Russian, but he'd lived here most of his life. His name had an Islamic ring to it, though, so I asked him about that. Sure enough, he was Muslim.

By then, we'd been joking around, and I felt free to say, "Are you kidding me? You're a terrible Muslim. You're drinking; you got your girlfriend pregnant. You can't be a Muslim!"

"I'm a Muslim at heart," he said, not taking offense at all. He told me his fiancée was a Christian. He opened up and talked about his worries about marriage and parenthood. I told him my story and explained what it would mean to follow Jesus—not just in his heart but also in every way.

I asked him if the baby was going to be a Muslim or a Christian. We talked about that for a while, then I told him, "You know, at some point you're gonna have to decide about your faith."

He did not make a decision right then and there on the plane, but he took in everything I said and has continued to consider it. I know that because we've stayed in touch. Someday I'd love to get a call from him telling me he's finally decided to follow Jesus.

This encounter with my Russian Muslim friend reminds me that what I think is someone's context may not be anywhere close. But sometimes all it takes for God to do something big and mysterious is to stay tuned in to the Holy Spirit, to draw in his perfect noticing ability.

Not long ago, I made it through security with my clothes still on and even had time to grab a bite to eat. I stopped to get sushi before boarding my plane at the Charlotte airport. I usually take food to the gate and eat it there, but I had time to kill, so I sat in the restaurant. My waitress noticed that my hand was in a cast and commented on it. Well, there wasn't a story there, at least not an impressive one. She told me her sister had recently been in an accident. Her face crumpled a bit, and she added, "She lost her entire arm."

Here's where this story gets interesting. Early one morning the week before, I'd read a story in our local newspaper about a girl who was involved in a boating accident at Lake Norman and lost her arm. I hardly ever read that paper. And I don't remember the last time I did this, but as soon as I read it, I prayed right then and there for that girl and for her family. I said to the Lord, *If there's any way I can help this family, would you make it happen?* Then I kind of forgot about it. Until the morning a week later in the airport.

Imagine how my waitress felt when she heard I had been praying for her a week before we met? She wasn't impressed with me; she was impressed with God. She was awed that he noticed her. And then she started saying the kinds of things people say when they talk about God in depth for the first time.

"I used to go to church, but I don't now."

I saw right then that God had orchestrated this moment, not just for the girl who had had the accident but for her sister who was right here in front of me. I told her I had a message for her, and, in that God-engineered context, she was ready to hear it:

"God wants me to tell you that he misses you. He wants you back."

When Jesus stopped and noticed one woman in a crowd, he did it for us too. He did it to illustrate that we are called to live like he did, to stop and create divine *kairos* (opportune) moments. To heal people. To slow down long enough to anticipate those moments. As people brush up against us day after day, to do what he did:

Stop.

Notice.

Touch.

Speak.

It's time we started acting and believing as if the Spirit of God lives in us, because he does. He has the words of life, and if we'll let him, he can use us to give that life to others. It's time to move on. Don't get stuck being the woman who touched Jesus' hem. Own being Jesus.

My Context: Never Foreign to God

Contrary to some of the bad theology you may have heard out there, Jesus is not American. (In fact, the odds are he probably looked a whole lot more like me than like the average American.) The church in the United States does not have dibs on the gospel. But for me, this American soil is the context where I needed to be to finally hear and respond to Jesus. That doesn't mean God wasn't aware of me or wooing me when I lived in Kuwait. Mahmood's declaration that he was a Christian may have been my first personal encounter with Christianity, but it wasn't the first time God worked in my life. That's because he can work in any context.

FOURTEEN

WHAT IF EVERYONE

And the King will answer them, "Truly, I say to you,
as you did it to one of the least of these my brothers,
you did it to me."

—MATTHEW 25:40

BECAUSE I'M PAKISTANI PEOPLE OFTEN assume that I was born there or even that I grew up there. This assumption leads to another one: that I grew up in third-world poverty. But nothing could be further from the truth. I was born in Kuwait and lived there until I came to the States at the ripe age of seventeen, almost eighteen. I visited Pakistan only once until my last visit when my mom was deported there. Even so, most people still imagine that I grew up poor and was educated in the school of hard knocks.

It seems to me these presuppositions are like thinking everyone from Nashville, Tennessee, is a country-music singer or that everyone from Texas is a rancher or a cowpoke (what is that, anyway?). Or that all Americans are rude. We Middle

Easterners get used to profiling. But let me use a few numbers to put things from my part of the world in perspective.

The United Nations uses a "score" known as the Human Development Index to serve as a frame of reference for social and economic development.[1] The index is calculated based on a country's gross national product, its average life expectancy at birth and other health measurements, and its educational records. Contrary to what you might think, the United States is not number one on this list. It's third, behind Norway and Australia. There are four brackets in the index: very high, high, medium, and low human development. Kuwait's number is fifty-four, at the top end of the "high" bracket. Pakistan's is 146, which indicates a low level of human development.

Kuwait is a rich country. Like the United States, especially in the years before our latest economic downturn, Kuwait has offered opportunities galore for upward mobility. Kuwait and Pakistan may be in the same hemisphere, but geography is where the similarities between them end. Except for climate and geography, they are as different as the North Pole is from the equator.

Islam operates differently in Pakistan than in Kuwait. According to Operation World, Kuwait's population is 13.79 percent Christian, and 38 percent of its people are unreached with the gospel.[2] On paper, Kuwait's laws look similar to Pakistan's. An inherited, constitutional emirate, Kuwait is ruled by the Sheikh's Sunni Muslim family. There are blasphemy laws on the books just like in Pakistan, but in practice Kuwait is far more lenient, offering more acquittals than prison sentences to offenders. You can still get arrested for maligning Islam or the Qu'ran, but this is much less likely in

Kuwait than in Pakistan. Christians enjoy relative freedom there.

By comparison Pakistan is heavily influenced by Sharia law, especially the laws that prohibit Muslims from converting to Christianity. The population is 97 percent unreached and a mere 2.45 percent Christian.[3] If current trends remain in place, Christians in Pakistan are in for more persecution than they've already endured. According to a recent survey of voters between the ages of eighteen and twenty-nine, many young people believe Pakistan's mixture of democracy and Sharia law has been disastrous. And they're all for chucking the democracy part. Raza Rumi, an Islamabad-based writer and analyst, credits this thinking to "a really confused young population that is brainwashed with visions of a glorious Islamic past and the gritty reality of unemployment, insecurity and political turmoil."[4] If the situations in other countries that are completely ruled by Sharia law are any indication, the fate of Christians in Pakistan could become even more dismal.

MOVING AWAY OR MOVING TOWARD

I never experienced any of this—religious intolerance, persecution, poverty, political unrest, and suffering—firsthand. War, yes. But even that was nothing like the horrors of war most people experience in other countries, where deadly conflict stretches into decades and corpses line the sides of their roads. No, I haven't suffered. Not in Kuwait and certainly not here in the States. So what's my point? That I was a privileged, spoiled kid in the Middle East, and I'm a privileged, spoiled adult in the United States? Well, I guess that could be true, but my point is that suffering and I have never gotten along.

I mentioned the naked, little boy I saw from the safe distance of my rickshaw on an early visit to Pakistan. He was playing in the gutters of Lahore, and when I locked eyes with him for a brief moment, I concluded that I never, ever wanted to be him. I would never be poor. That was a pivotal moment for me. I have spent much of my life, probably more than my brothers or sisters, running away from poverty. I like nice things. I want to be secure. Heck, I'm not a sheikh—though a few people have asked me about that—but I've always wanted to be rich. Strange ambition for a pastor, right? Well, at first I had no reason to doubt my desire for wealth and comfort. I bought into a theology that said if you followed Jesus you would move away from suffering and lack of any kind. In fact, prosperity was a sure sign that you were blessed. Suffering meant something was amiss in your spiritual life. For a while I just assumed it was really convenient that God and I both wanted the same thing.

Today, when I meet successful entrepreneurs, I'll often discover that they grew up with nothing, and early in life they determined to never live that way again, to make absolutely certain their family didn't experience the poverty that defined their early years. They want nothing to do with suffering or lack. Self-sufficiency is their highest value. I understand this line of reasoning. Suffering is no fun. Poverty is no fun. Why would any of us choose that?

But here's the weird thing about suffering: as much as I want to avoid it, in a sick way I'm also drawn to it. Go ahead and admit it: you are too. I mean, why else are there seven *Saw* movies? Why are there well over a hundred thousand views of Louisville basketball player Kevin Ware's infamous and gruesome broken leg incident on YouTube? I never went to a *Saw* movie, but I did catch a glimpse of Kevin Ware's horrendous injury . . . through my fingers as I tried not to look but couldn't help it. And I slow down to look at a wreck even when it is on the other side of the median. I think I need therapy. Most of us have this unhealthy fascination with suffering. As long as we can remain spectators, that is.

Even though we want to view suffering, we'd rather see it from a distance—on our way out the door or receding in our rearview mirrors. As human and maybe even as normal as this is, I have become convinced it is not at all like Jesus. Even weirder than our strange fascination with suffering is Jesus' example. Instead of staying away from suffering, Jesus seemed resolved to move toward it every time. I've finally determined that if I am going to be like him, to follow him in every way imaginable, I will do the same. I will move intentionally and confidently toward pain and suffering and lack in order to comfort and heal and help. If I'm going to have a life that looks like Jesus', this trajectory is unavoidable.

MISSION STATEMENT

Somewhere around Jesus' thirtieth birthday, he launched into his formal ministry. He traveled around doing God things and calling his followers to come behind him and learn to do the same. Jesus never once guaranteed them suffering-free lives. He never claimed he would lead his followers away from suffering. He was clear about that. One day in the first few months of his ministry, he entered the synagogue in his hometown of Nazareth; because he was already considered a Rabbi, he was allowed to read the Scripture. He opened the scroll of Isaiah and read these verses:

> The Spirit of the Lord is upon me, because he has anointed me to proclaim good news to the poor. He has sent me to proclaim liberty to the captives and recovering of sight to the blind, to set at liberty those who are oppressed, to proclaim the year of the Lord's favor. (Luke 4:18–19)

This was, in effect, Jesus' mission statement: to move toward those who suffer in order to comfort them, to help them, and to heal them. This is at the heart of the incarnation. Jesus divested himself of the perks of royalty, one of which was the privilege of avoiding personal suffering and even the suffering of others. A king could go so far as to prohibit anyone from having a bad mood in his presence! But Jesus was not that kind of king. In every possible way, including in our suffering, pain, loss, and lack, he became one of us. And this is the heart of the gospel. Jesus entered into our suffering so that we might never experience the ultimate suffering of separation from his Father. If this was his mission statement, to run straight toward the suffering of others, then how can it not be ours as well?

Typically a mission statement is immediately followed by action points. Steps to ensure that our lives move in the direction of our missions. I'm not opposed to action points, but Jesus' approach was a little different. Later on in Luke, a lawyer approached him and asked him, "Teacher, what shall I do to inherit eternal life?" (Luke 10:25). This was a case of quid pro quo, a question that was essentially, "What do I do to get what? What are my action steps, Jesus?"

As he often did, Jesus countered this question with another question: "What is written in the Law? How do you read it?" (v. 26).

The man didn't skip a beat and quoted the Jewish *Shema* from Deuteronomy 6:5, a passage every good Jew quoted each morning and placed strategically above the doorway of his house: "You shall love the Lord your God with all your heart and with all your soul and with all your strength and with all your mind, and your neighbor as yourself" (v. 27).

It was a stock answer, but a good one, and Jesus affirmed it. But the lawyer was stuck on quid pro quo. He wanted clear, measurable, attainable action steps. What mattered most to him was getting to the final outcome of eternal life by doing whatever he was supposed to do. He asked Jesus, "And who is my neighbor?" (v. 29). He's like, "Give me the list to check off Jesus, because I can knock this out."

The lawyer must have been a little put off by the story Jesus told him next in lieu of a straight-up answer to his question. To tell the truth, I have always been intrigued by the story of the good Samaritan. That's because Jesus refused to give action steps that lead to eternal life. He didn't detail a how-to list of ways to get to eternal life. No ten easy steps into the kingdom of God here. Instead, Jesus described the kind of person who has eternal life. And it's a pretty unsettling picture. The story itself started out very conventionally. The road from Jerusalem to Jericho was known for muggings and murders. Back then people called it the Bloody Path.[5] There were probably people in the crowd who whispered to one another, "Oh yeah, that same thing happened to my cousin last year," or "I heard the violence on that road has gotten even worse."

The first two men in Jesus' story were traveling from Jerusalem back home to Jericho. This is an important detail. It means their work at the temple was done. If they'd been going the other direction, almost no one would fault them for avoiding the "unclean" Samaritan because everyone understood the need for a priest or temple official to remain pure before performing temple duties. But these men were going home. They could have risked impurity much more readily for the sake of a suffering man. If they'd wanted to, that is. I've done the same thing more times than I can count when I've seen a homeless man holding a cardboard sign at an intersection; they both avoided eye contact and changed lanes. If cell phones had been invented, they might have held theirs to their ears and pretended they were on a call. Anything to avoid responsibility for the heap of blood and bones on the side of the road.

Like the theology I used to believe in, man-made tradition in those days held that proximity to suffering equaled fewer blessings. This is why it was such a big deal when Jesus touched the lepers he healed. And this is why the fact that a despised Samaritan chose to intervene when the good Jews didn't was such a dramatic twist in this story. Have you ever noticed that at the end of the story, when Jesus asked which man was a neighbor, the lawyer said, "The man who showed him mercy" instead of "the Samaritan"? It's likely that he couldn't bring himself to utter such a name. The label *Samaritan* represented the most despicable person—the one you could hardly stomach, much less love. And here Jesus said this man was the epitome of a neighbor. And, just as likely, when Jesus said, "You go, and do likewise," it felt like a slap on the face to the Jews in the crowd (Luke 10:37).

What he said, essentially, was this: "You go and be a Samaritan. Be the lowest of the low serving the poorest and neediest of the poor and needy."

I'm sure the man thought, *Jesus, give me some easy action steps instead, because I'm not sure I can be this kind of person.* The Samaritan was not rich, yet he sacrificed radically by giving a full two-days' wages to cover the man's expenses. He moved intentionally toward suffering, pain, and lack to comfort, heal, and help. That's what it looks like to live out eternal life. My urge to have is replaced by an urge to give. My life begins to reflect Paul's description in 2 Corinthians 1:3–4: "Blessed be the God and Father of our Lord Jesus Christ, the Father of mercies and God of all comfort, who comforts us in all our affliction, so that we may be able to comfort those who are in any affliction, with the comfort with which we ourselves are comforted by God." My craving for comfort is replaced by a craving to comfort others. If I see a person in need, I *have* to do something about it. I don't avoid pain, I run to it (1 John 3:17). Over and over and over.

I have to confess that I don't have this down yet. But I do know that I could spend my whole life reciting, learning, and dissecting Scripture, but if I'm not the kind of person who oozes eternal life like this, then I'm not a true follower. Staying in step with Jesus doesn't mean getting it right; it means loving people the way God loves them.

WIE: "What If Everyone"

Ashley and I are definitely works in progress in this area. And, as we grow in this kingdom value of running straight toward suffering and lack instead of away from it, Mosaic is growing too. We're learning a lot from each other. Ashley, unlike her shallow, wannabe-rich husband, has always had a heart for outreach to those in need. She was on a mission before I had a clue what the word meant. Her early forays into the needs of others took the form of mission trips, but that was often unsatisfying because, while they taught her a lot, she couldn't figure out how to do missions on a more consistent, daily basis. Ashley would say she's not a leader, but I beg to differ. She knows how to feel deeply, take responsibility, inspire others, and make things happen. She goes about it quietly, with steely determination.

Not long after we planted Mosaic, Ashley had our daughter, Nurah. A new baby and a toddler in the house did not make for much productivity anywhere else but at home. But God was stirring in Ashley's heart. We both agreed that we wanted Mosaic to have a strong outreach component, but in that first year there just wasn't anyone who had the passion or the know-how to get it done. And Ashley was occupied.

Early in 2009, Nurah was out of diapers, and Ashley was out of the baby fog and ready to get out of the house. If my wife is anything, she's purposeful, so "out of the house" did not translate into aerobics and tennis. During this time she went on a road trip with friends, and, along the way, she swiped a book she saw at the top of a stack at a friend's house (don't worry, she asked permission to take it). It was Shane Claiborne's *The*

Irresistible Revolution. For the rest of her trip, she devoured the book. It shook her to her core so much that she dragged me with her to Davidson College to hear him speak a few months later. His message about suffering and how the church has avoided it for far too long shook me as well.

In the meantime, Ashley's parents' church in Seneca, South Carolina, started an outreach deal where they'd clean up neighborhoods and parks around town, and it got Ashley's creative juices flowing. She read more books and did more research, and before long she was ready to do something at Mosaic. She didn't know what, but it was time to take action, and I agreed. Ashley began to talk with people at Mosaic and in our community who had a similar passion. They decided to start a nonprofit organization that was loosely a part of Mosaic. The initial plan was to involve other area churches in local service days, like the ones in Seneca or Fellowship Bible in Little Rock. We had our first service event in 2009, and as of this writing, we've done a total of eight. This past spring, beginning with a community rally, we did Seven Days of Service, which included groups like Love, Inc., national relief organizations like Citi Impact, global efforts like African Children's Project, and many more.

They started calling this project What If Everyone, and it has been a group effort from the get-go. They did not copy a specific template, and their model hasn't been static. It has continually evolved since its inception in 2009. Ashley and her group of leaders discovered that the bigger churches in our community—the ones with formidable resources—were less likely to join in because many of them were doing their own service projects. They also found that one great entrée into the community is partnering with secular businesses. Our events are on the local Starbucks' website; the mayor of our part of Charlotte, Huntersville, showed up at our most recent rally; and the firemen we served have connected with us. This approach, a less in-the-church-bubble approach, is more in line with the vision of Mosaic. Instead of fostering an us-ministering-to-them mentality, we've become a more organic part of the neighborhood. It has enabled us to penetrate our community on a deeper, more personal level.

I'm thankful we've become so integrally engaged with our community. I love the fact that the crowd that typically gathers at our WIE rallies more accurately reflects the community than the church, including people of many ethnicities, gays, agnostics, atheists, and the working poor. After being here a few years, we found that while we don't have a lot of urban issues within a ten-mile radius of the school where we meet as a church, we do have plenty of people who are barely making ends meet, who live paycheck to paycheck. They are our neighbors, so we have tailored much of what we do through What If Everyone to meet their particular needs. And we've gotten over-the-top creative in the process.

WIE has enabled us to penetrate the world around us, but it has also penetrated us from within. If you ask people at our church what they love most about Mosaic, many of them will say What If Everyone. Neither Ashley nor I, when we first started in 2009, had any idea how essential WIE would become to the ministry of Mosaic.

What If Everyone has transformed our vision for Mosaic in multiple ways. We've been meeting in a local high school for longer than any of us would choose, and we recently launched a building-fund campaign. Not owning a building at first was, by the way, our strategy—not just a necessity. We knew the day would come when God would show us when it was time to own our own place. In today's age of nomadic churches who don't own real estate, I know there are many of you out there who can relate to the weekly grind of setting up portable nurseries and sound systems and welcome centers, only to dismantle them until next Sunday. We have an amazing team of volunteers who pull it off with excellence week after week, but to be honest we're all getting a little tired of pipe-and-drape and dropping our kids off in a high school cafeteria, no matter how beautifully transformed it may be. The limitations of this setup are many. I think we can safely say that we *need* a building.

But this goes way beyond a need. We began with a dream to be a church full of people who live by faith, who are known by their love, and who are a voice of hope. What started as a vision to create a diverse church where people can belong before they believe is evolving before our eyes as we listen to God and seek to follow his lead. What he has in store for us is so much more than a building. It's an opportunity—a power tool for his purposes. We want to create and outfit a space to grow our community and serve our city. And God has stretched our imaginations to see this as:

- A safe and secure environment for our kids to be taught and loved and for our youth to gather;
- A place to grow our current ministries, worship, leadership training, and discipleship;
- A headquarters for outreach to the city;

- A distribution center of hope, where we can collect items for those in need, house those who need shelter, feed the hungry, and provide financial support and job training for the working poor.

The way I figure it, if we cannot follow Jesus personally without intentionally and consistently moving toward suffering and lack, if loving like God loves means helping and comforting and healing those who are in pain, then shouldn't any building we build have a similar purpose?

FIFTEEN

An Invitation to an Unconquerable Life

To one who has faith, no explanation is necessary.
To one without faith, no explanation is possible.
— attributed to Saint Thomas Aquinas

I know for some there is the question that's been bugging you since the first chapter. It's been such a distraction that you may have even put the book down to do a quick Google image search just to satisfy your curiosity. I understand. I owe it to you to answer it, as dumb a question as it is. Maybe I never should have mentioned it at all, but I think it adds some flair to my story. Okay, here goes: no, Ashley is not blonde. (Well, sometimes she is.)

For those of you who didn't pay attention, I'll remind you that one of my primary goals when I first came to the States was to meet blonde women. And then I landed in Miami where everyone looked like me, dark hair and all. It was a major disappointment at the time.

As silly as it may seem to bring this up here, or at all for that matter, it makes an important point. Three weeks after the day I landed in a sea of brunettes at Miami International Airport, my goals in life did a complete U-turn. What once mattered most to me no longer mattered the same or at all. Ashley is beautiful—a total hottie. But while I appreciate the way she looks *a lot*, her inner, imperishable beauty matters to me more. Meeting Jesus did that to me; it turned me into a guy who cared more about the things that are going to last forever that I cannot see than about the things that will eventually fade that I can see.

Inner. Imperishable. Until I met Christ, those were foreign concepts to me.

I've Met Him

Not long ago a young Palestinian woman came to Mosaic, brought to the Sunday morning service by a friend. Afterward, before I could get from the front of the building to the lobby, she pulled me aside, locked blazing, dark eyes on me, and said, "You have a really interesting story."

I thanked her and then paused so she could continue. There was something about her. I could tell there was a deeper question buried in her comment, and my hunch was right. "I want to know why you would leave Islam and follow Jesus."

"Are you a Muslim?" I asked.

"Yes," she said.

I knew it. We exchanged contact information and set up a time for her to come by the church office later in the week. Thirty minutes before the day and time for her appointment, the office cleared out completely. I immediately began strategizing about how I was going to move our meeting to somewhere else. I don't relish being alone in the office with any woman other than my wife, especially a Muslim woman. But I didn't have to worry; she'd brought her cousin along. Actually, by the looks of him, she'd brought a bodyguard.

Other than a brusque greeting, he was silent while she and I chitchatted a little, asking about each other's families and backgrounds. I have to admit that this guy—without saying a word—was intimidating. He was Middle Eastern to the core, and he looked like he could take me, if you know what I'm saying. I wasn't sure why he was there other than as backup. I wondered, *Am I that scary?*

After a while I directed our conversation away from the small talk to Jesus. And then her friend went from stone-faced to animated in sixty seconds flat. "What kind of Christian are you?" he challenged me.

I wasn't sure what he meant. I didn't have to wonder for long, because he followed up with, "Are you one of those Jerry Falwell Christians?"

I must have looked puzzled, because he added, "Are you, you know, a Muslim-hater?"

I answered that loaded question as best I could. I did a little PR work for the mislabeled "Jerry Falwell Christians" out there, but I explained that hating Muslims wasn't the way of Jesus. I explained that I had nothing at all against Muslims, but that I didn't believe their claims were accurate. With that out of the way, the three of us launched into—believe it or not—a very friendly debate.

Our conversation centered mostly on the differences between the Qu'ran and the Bible. I've already referred to the tenacious belief most Muslims hold that the Qu'ran is more pure and reliable than the Bible because one man wrote it, as opposed to the multiple authors who penned the Bible. We talked about the various claims about how Muslims ended up with their Qu'ran. Some assert that Muhammad wrote it, and others say it was delivered by the angel Gabriel. History tells us Muhammad spent a lot of time with Jewish Christians, so we discussed the elements of the Torah that are woven throughout his book.

It was a stimulating discussion, and I was convinced all three of us were having a good time. Finally, I stopped and said, "You know, we could do this all day long. We could debate our holy books and our histories. We could dig into them and talk about their claims in great detail. We could compare Muhammad to Jesus."

"But here's the thing," I told them, "I have met him."

Who can argue with that?

Before they left I thanked them for being people who seek the truth, who are concerned about a deeper meaning to this life. I told them I appreciated that they were very spiritual. I then challenged them to see Jesus, the person. To ask him to reveal himself to them. I told them he was waiting to be found by them. They left moved; I could see it.

As you know, Christians and family members and Muslims and Hindus and agnostics and atheists—the people I know and love and the acquaintances I've met—have indeed argued that what happened to me in my brother's apartment all those years ago was not proof of anything other than my mentally instability.

When people hear my story, they have the prerogative to dismiss it or believe it, and many have done both. But this book is not a defense of my story. It is not even a defense of Jesus.

If anything, this book is a resounding echo of that statement: I have met him.

I have met him, so I know he is fully capable of defending himself. (I find it interesting that in the Psalms every single time the words *defense* or *defender* are used, they refer to God, not to us.)

I have met him, so I know who he is more intimately than I know the facts about him.

I have met him, which means I have experienced the benefits of knowing him: healing, transformation, and power.

I have not only met him; I have heard him speak to me on multiple occasions. And I passionately believe that you can meet him and hear him speak too.

If Christianity says anything, it is this: we can meet God in Jesus. He is seeking just this—to meet us. And if we ask, he'll show up in our lives and speak to us.

And when he does, we can echo John's words:

That which was from the beginning, which we have heard, which we have seen with our eyes, which we looked upon and have touched with our hands, concerning the word of life—the life was made manifest, and we have seen it, and testify to it and proclaim to you the eternal life, which was with the Father and was made manifest to us—that which we have seen and heard we proclaim also to you, so that you too may have fellowship with us; and indeed our fellowship is with the Father and with his Son Jesus Christ. And we are writing these things so that our joy may be complete. (1 John 1:1–4)

INDESCRIBABLE

It's funny how two people can see the same thing and describe it in completely opposite ways. Like my first vision of Jesus. When I told others about seeing him, many of them did not see his imperishable, overwhelming, eternal beauty in my story. What they saw was a crazy guy's delusions or a sincere guy's exaggerations. That used to frustrate me a lot more than it does now.

Not only is it not my job to defend what is true; I've come to realize that this is simply the nature of the best things in life. You can't tell people about them.

Well, you can, but they will not fully grasp what you tell them by your description alone. Take the sugary, caffeinated goodness of a hazelnut Frappuccino. Even if I possessed the skills of a Madison Avenue ad executive or the persuasive prowess of a big-shot litigation attorney, I could never adequately convince you that it tastes amazing.

You'd have to pick one up and take a sip of it for yourself to get what I'm saying. Adjectives are just so inadequate. I know it's a silly example, but it's a good one.

My story not only describes an encounter with Jesus Christ; it also makes the case that God could very well be speaking to you just as he did to me. I'll wager he is. Conversations with

God always have a purpose embedded in them: his purpose. God doesn't just say things to us. He presents opportunities to us. And the only way we will really get to experience those opportunities is if we pick them up and take a sip of them for ourselves. We have to enter into them by risking to believe. My experience tells me that the opportunities God offers us usually require more faith than we have at the time. They stretch our little faith to larger proportions than we thought possible.

Of course I did not know any of this back then. I just knew that Jesus revealed himself to me and that my life no longer belonged to me. That's where the faith part came in. Seeing Jesus was hard to deny. In fact, it would have taken more faith on my part *not* to believe what I saw. But trusting him with the trajectory of my life from that point on was an entirely different story. Little did I know that I was embarking on a lifelong journey of soul-stretching faith.

What's in a Name?

The people in Scripture who by faith picked up the opportunities God gave them and drank are famous today, thousands of years later. Theirs are the names we remember. Take Caleb and Joshua. Stop for a minute, and take an inventory of how many Calebs or Joshuas or Joshes you know. More than a couple, I bet. These names never go out of style. Now, how about Shammua or Shapat or Palti? *Wait a minute, Naeem,* you may be thinking, *those are weird, Middle Eastern names. The names Caleb and Joshua are as American as a two-ton pickup truck.*

I hate to break it to you, but the names Joshua and Caleb

are no less Middle Eastern than Shammua or Palti. There's a good reason these two names survived and the others didn't, and that reason has everything to do with faith.

At the very edge of the promised land, God spoke to his people with a clear purpose in mind. He gave them an opportunity that would stretch their faith, and Joshua and Caleb were the only two besides Moses and Aaron who trusted him enough to pick it up and drink it. Their story in Numbers 13 isn't the only one like it in the Bible. There are plenty of other examples where God presented a big idea to average men and women just like us—an idea of something he wanted to do in and through them. He stretched their imaginations, and I'm thankful that someone wrote it down for posterity so we could learn from their examples. I guess you could say much of the Bible is simply the record of men and women who articulated the conversations they had with God.

Here's something to consider: what if the only difference between the life you want to live and the life you're currently living is that you've never written down anything God has said to you? I don't mean to suggest that using a pen on paper is a magic faith trick or anything like that. But I have noticed that if I don't articulate an important idea from God, I usually don't act on it. Writing it down is an effective way to start the faith ball rolling. And not writing it down is an easy way to avoid acting on it. Either way, if you write it on paper, state it out loud, or seal it in conversation, faith steps must be articulated.

Although I advocate not pressuring Muslims with the gospel, once the conversation has begun, I'll often challenge them with the thought that the day will come when they'll need to make a decision. Another way to say that is, the day will come when they will need to choose or deny faith, and then to act on that decision.

When Jesus did a miracle, he often asked the person if he or she wanted it first. He forced him or her to articulate his or her choice. "What do you want me to do for you?" (Luke 18:41) he asked the blind man, or "Do you want to be healed?" (John 5:6) to the lame man. He did not pressure them to have faith, but once they had even a whiff of it, he impressed on them how important it was to express in words whatever God wanted to accomplish in them and through them.

Could it be the reason you are discouraged about your life today is that in that moment when God wanted to stretch your faith, you took a pass? The defining moment came and left without you taking one step into it. Either you had a decision to make and went the other direction, or you simply defaulted by not choosing anything at all.

This decision aspect of faith is never clearer in the geography of the Bible than right at the border of the promised land. Moses reminded the people that God had spoken to them time and time again about what was going to happen next. God's direction was clear, but the way was not wide open. There was a big "No Trespassing" sign on it. We often think that when God speaks, the next step will be into wide-open access to the dream. But it's never like that.

Moses called together twelve men, one from each tribe, and sent them out as spies to scope out the land. This was their defining moment, in which they would have to choose to step into the very reason they left Egypt in the first place, or to walk away from it. The twelve men came back after a month and a half in enemy territory and said, "We came to the land to which you sent us. It flows with milk and honey, and this is its fruit. However . . ." (Num. 13:27–28).

The deadly "however." Ten guys with names that were destined for obscurity said:

> However, the people who dwell in the land are strong, and the cities are fortified and very large. And besides, we saw the descendants of Anak there. The Amalekites dwell in the land of the Negeb. The Hittites, the Jebusites, and the Amorites dwell in the hill country. And the Canaanites dwell by the sea, and along the Jordan. (Num. 13:28–29)

Grasshopper Theology

When Caleb challenged this view of things and urged the people to "go up at once and occupy it, for we are well able to overcome it" (v. 30), the other ten spies counter-argued with even more vehemence, not just voicing their concerns to Moses, but spreading a "bad report" throughout the camp:

> The land, through which we have gone to spy it out, is a land that devours its inhabitants, and all the people that we saw in it are of great height. And there we saw the Nephilim (the sons of Anak, who come from the Nephilim), and we seemed to ourselves like grasshoppers, and so we seemed to them. (vv. 32–33)

Have you ever had a dream that was big enough to make you small? Insecurity, unbelief, and fear can paralyze us so that the big idea God has given us becomes impossible in our eyes and makes us feel like grasshoppers. The people wept aloud all night long so that their voices rose in a chorus of dissent against Moses. They'd determined the vision was absolutely insane. They started saying things like, "Why is the LORD bringing us into this land, to fall by the sword? Our wives and our little ones will become a prey. Would it not be better for us to go back to Egypt?" (Num. 14:3), which could be roughly translated, "We are so afraid of this opportunity, we might as well be slaves for another hundred years."

This was more serious than a little whining; it carried a lot more weight with God. He asked Moses, "How long will this people despise me?" (v. 11). Moses and Aaron fell facedown on the ground when they heard this. Joshua and Caleb tore their clothes. They addressed the people and challenged them to remember God's promise. His favor was on them and had been from Egypt until this pivotal place in their history. The land was theirs. "Don't be afraid. Step up and enter in." I can imagine that this was a real *Braveheart* moment.

But it didn't end well. The people responded by picking up stones to kill them, to shut them up. In response God told the people through Moses that they could have what they wanted—the ultimate punishment—and that they would surely not enter the promised land. Everyone who believed the lie would die, but their descendants, plus Joshua and Caleb, would be allowed to enter. God made good on this promise, and the ten men who fostered lies about God and about his plans died prematurely as a result of a plague.

"Wait a minute," the people said, "that's not what we had in mind either, God." The Scriptures tell us they mourned, but instead of repenting before the Lord, they took matters into their own hands. What happened next may look like faith, but it wasn't. The people, acting on their grief and fear and guilt, charged into the hill country of their enemies, ignoring Moses' warning: "Why now are you transgressing the command of the LORD, when that will not succeed? Do not go up, for the Lord is not among you, lest you be struck down before your enemies" (Num. 14:41–42).

It was a disaster. They were beaten, and badly. These Israelites thought, like I have too often, that the secret to life was found in their control. Once I've figured things out by my reasoning, I think I'll move forward. But I have learned it's always a bad idea to trust in my own reasoning. It may be painful to allow God to stretch my faith, but it is worth it every single time.

BENEDICTION

Every Sunday at Mosaic, we read the same verses at the end of the service. You could call it our benediction, which is about as traditional as it gets around here. The word *benediction* is an old one—about five hundred years old or more—derived from two Latin words: *benedicere*, which means "to bless," and *dicereto*, "to say."[1] Put them together, and it means "to speak well of." Our benediction speaks well of God, but it also speaks well of what he will do through us if we will only believe him. Here's the truth that we proclaim out loud together every week:

> Now to him who is able to do far more abundantly than
> all that we ask or think, according to the power at work
> within us, to him be glory in the church and in Christ
> Jesus throughout all generations, forever and ever. Amen.
> (Eph. 3:20–21)

If you think about it, this is a subversive agenda. It promises something only an invisible, powerful, *real* God can do. It means that God, who speaks to us, might really be able to do the things he says he will do. That he will not only do them, but he'll do them better, more lavishly, more fully, and more powerfully than we could ever imagine with our finite minds. It means that faith in what God has to say must be, by definition, something that stretches our known world beyond what is humanly possible.

Every week I pray that someone really believes it.

By now I'm sure you realize that my story is more than a supernatural tale involving demons in which Jesus showed up on cue to vanquish the enemies. It's even more than the account of a Muslim guy leaving Islam for Jesus. Compared to the rest of the story—the flight path of my life from that first day until now—the first chapter of this book was a brief interlude. A flicker in time. But, you may be thinking, *At least you had that, Naeem. I have never seen Jesus. Never had that kind of experience.*

I hear you, and so does he.

The writer of Hebrews refers to "a great cloud of witnesses" surrounding us as we start, continue, and finish this life of faith (12:1 NIV). It's such a vivid picture. It evokes something we all need but often never have: a group of raving fans who cheer us on when the going gets tough. The thing is, whether you see them or not, they are there. And I confess that I have never, not once, seen these witnesses, who I assume are the saints of old, who have gone before us. In the same way, whether you have seen him or not, Jesus was, is, and will be present in your life. And if you do what Mahmood encouraged me to do and ask him to reveal himself to you, he will. One way or another, he will.

The events in the first chapter of this book represent a miniscule pinpoint in time. If I counted up the seconds, the minutes, or the days when I actually had empirical evidence that Jesus was present in my own life, they would add up to less than half an hour or so. That's not a lot of time compared to the almost forty years of my life so far. But the times he has actually been there, present and alive, add up to my entire lifetime. Yours too.

My story is not over yet. What started with an ordinary prayer led to an extraordinary story, and to a life that is not my own.

Your story isn't over yet either.

What if you simply asked God to reveal himself to you? Could it be that God is whispering to your soul? Could he be waiting for you to take a step into something that exists only in his imagination, something he can and will do through his "power at work" in you (Eph. 3:20)?

Take a step into an extraordinary life with an ordinary prayer.

Don't keep him waiting.

Afterword

How do I describe my friend Naeem Fazal?

Inquisitive? Passionate? Creative? Cool? Intriguing? Spiritual? Funny? Visionary? Leader?

He is all those things, but so much more. He is a unique creation of God. A passionate follower of Christ with a story so refreshing and unusual that I'm sure it kept you turning the pages. His story comes without the usual baggage of those of us raised in a Christian culture, although, after an initial supernatural encounter with Jesus, he quickly got caught up in the trappings of doing church rather than pursuing a Savior. Fortunately for all of us, God is with us in the good, the bad, and the ugly. I love how Naeem didn't gloss over the seamier side of his journey, but showed us how God rewarded his very human but diligent seeking.

I love his story because, although we were born in very

different cultures, we have traveled amazingly similar journeys in our pursuit of God. I think you probably found some
of your story in his story. Hopefully it has encouraged you to
see God as more than a concept, but as a living breathing reality, desiring to step into your daily routine, challenging your
preconceived ideas of who he is.

It's been my privilege to work with, walk with, and love
Naeem and Ashley for the past few years. They have been
influential in the faith of our children, and for that we will
be forever grateful. We've shared laughter and tears. Dreams
and a few heartaches. We've been used by God to shepherd
two great congregations of people. I see them as some of my
spiritual kids.

I remember the day Naeem came into my office to share
his dream of planting a church in Charlotte. When he asked
me what I thought I replied with something like this, "If you
can do anything else, do it. But if not, you'd better go ahead
and plant it."

What I meant was that church planting is the hardest but
most rewarding thing you can possibly do. You will love it and
hate it at the same time. It will take everything you have not to
walk away in the first few years when you face the inevitable
resistance of the enemy of your soul, who will often be dis-
guised as biting sheep, rabid Christians with an agenda and a
taste for shepherd. It will hurt. You will be tested. Better men
than either of us have folded under the pressure.

Inside I was halfway hoping he would stay and we could
continue this amazing journey called Seacoast together.

But Naeem had met the real enemy face-to-face early in his
journey with Christ. And he had defeated him by the power

that is in Jesus' name. It had shaped his view of what God was capable of. He was ready for the challenge.

I hope you encountered a living, breathing, powerful God as you read this book. I hope you got the sense of what he is capable of. And I hope you will abandon yourself to a passionate pursuit of him.

If you do, your journey could be scary good.

Kind of like Naeem's.

Greg Surratt

Pastor of Seacoast Church and author of *Ir-rev-rend: Christianity Without the Pretense. Faith Without the Façade*

ACKNOWLEDGMENTS

Thanks to Greg Surratt, Michael Morris, and Pastor Satish Raiborde for being spiritual fathers to me.

And to Erwin McManus, for forever marking my life.

Thank you, Tim and Beverly, for being amazing in-laws.

Thanks to Arvind Merwah for being a brother to me.

Thank you, Paul Alverson, for walking with me.

Todd and Shannon Phelps, I look forward to changing the world and growing old with you guys.

Kitti Murray, I could not have asked for a better collaborator.

Mark Sweeney, thank you for being my agent and friend and for believing in this project.

And many thanks to:

Mahmood, for leading me to Jesus.

Obea, for being a constant encourager to me.

Atiya, for your passion for Jesus.

Ali, for teaching me never to quit.

Asher and Nurah, for the joy you are to me.

And lastly to Ashley Roberson Fazal, the love of my life, thank you for loving me more than I deserve.

Notes

CHAPTER 2: MAHMOOD

1. Dumas Malone, *Jefferson and the Rights of Man*
   (Charlottesville, VA: University of Virginia Press, 2007), 370.
2. Widely attributed to Andy Stanley, www.twitter.com.

CHAPTER 4: LIFE INTERRUPTED

1. Desert Shield refers to the buildup of troops in anticipation
   of a war against Hussein. On January 15, 1991, Desert Storm
   became Desert Shield.
2. "1991: Tornado down," On This Day, *BBC News*, http://news
   .bbc.co.uk/onthisday/hi/witness/january/17/newsid_2641000
   /2641621.stm.
3. Ibid.
4. "1990: Iraq invades Kuwait," On This Day, *BBC News*, http://
   news.bbc.co.uk/onthisday/hi/dates/stories/august/2/newsid
   _2526000/2526937.stm.
5. Ibid.
6. Anita Singh, "The World's Richest Royals," *Telegraph*, August

21, 2008, http://www.telegraph.co.uk/news/worldnews/2598278
/The-worlds-richest-royals.html.

7. "War in the Gulf: The Iraqi Leader; Saddam Hussein's Speech
on the 'Withdrawal' of His Army from Kuwait" *New York
Times,* February 27, 1991, http://www.nytimes.com/1991/02
/27/world/war-gulf-iraqi-leader-saddam-hussein-s-speech
-withdrawal-his-army-kuwait.html?pagewanted=all&src=pm.

8. *Encyclopaedia Britannica Online,* s. v. "Kuwait," http://www
.britannica.com/EBchecked/topic/325644/Kuwait.

9. K. Gajendra Singh, "Propaganda Wars: The Decline and Fall of
Western Media," *South Asia Analysis Group*, February 24, 2003,
http://www.southasiaanalysis.org/paper615.

CHAPTER 5: STRANGER IN A STRANGE LAND, PART TWO

1. Dallas Willard, *Hearing God* (Downers Grove, IL: Inter-Varsity,
1999), 18.

2. Erwin McManus, *The Barbarian Way* (Nashville: Thomas
Nelson Publishers, 2005), 64–65.

CHAPTER 7: BOLLYWOOD ASPIRATIONS

1. Herbert Ellinger, *Hinduism (Basics),* (London: Bloomsbury T
& T Clark, 1996), 92.

2. Brian Campbell, *The Roman Army: 31BC - AD 337, A
Sourcebook* (London: Routledge Publishers, 1994), 6.

CHAPTER 8: CHURCH STORIES

1. A. W. Tozer, *The Pursuit of God* (Harrisburg, PA: Christian
Publications, Inc., 1982), 13.

2. T. Austin Sparks, *The School of Christ* (Lindale, Texas: World
Challenge, 2000), 2.

CHAPTER 10: HOPE FOR THE HOPELESS

1. YWAM Relief, "Pakistan Relief and Development Funds,"
2006, http://www.ywamrelief.org.uk/about.html.

2. Saad Khan, "Pakistan's Poverty Bomb and the Hypocrisy of

Elite Classes," *Huffington Post*, September 22, 2009, http://
www.huffingtonpost.com/saad-khan/pakistans-poverty-bomb
-an_b_292985.html.

CHAPTER 11: GROWING UP AND GETTING READY

1. Erwin McManus, *Chasing Daylight* (Nashville: Thomas Nelson, 2006), 90.
2. Erwin McManus, *Seizing Your Divine Moment* (Nashville: Thomas Nelson, 2006), 35.

CHAPTER 14: WHAT IF EVERYONE

1. "International Human Development Indicators," *Human Development Reports*, http://hdr.undp.org/en/statistics/.
2. "Kuwait," *Operation World*, http://www.operationworld.org /country/kuwa/owtext.html.
3. "Pakistan," *Operation World*, http://www.operationworld.org /paki.
4. Andrew Buncombe, "Pakistan's youth favour Sharia law and military rule over democratic governance," *The Independent*, April 3, 2013, http://www.independent.co.uk/news/world/asia /pakistans-youth-favour-sharia-law-and-military-rule-over -democratic-governance-8558165.html.
5. Martin Luther King, Jr., *A Knock at Midnight: Inspiration from the Great Sermons of Reverend Martin Luther King, Jr.*, eds. Peter Holloran and Clayton Carson (New York: Warner Books, 2000), 129.

CHAPTER 15: AN INVITATION TO AN UNCONQUERABLE LIFE

1. Online Etymology Dictionary, s.v. *benediction*, http://www .etymonline.com/index.php?search=benediction.

About the Author

Naemm Fazal, a Pakistani, was born and raised as a Muslim in Kuwait. He came to the United States shortly after the Gulf War of 1990. In 1992, he had a supernatural experience with Jesus that changed the course of his life. In 2006, he planted Mosaic Church in Charlotte, North Carolina. He is also the cofounder of Charlotte's citywide outreach initiative, What If Everyone. Naeem has been featured in several magazines and on Christian networks. He often speaks at conferences and churches. For more on Naeem, please visit NaeemFazal.com, find him on Facebook, or follow him on Twitter (@naeemfazal) and Instagram (naeemfazal).

ABOUT KITTI MURRAY

Kitti Murray and her husband, Bill, live in a refugee community on the ragged edges of Atlanta, Georgia, that *Time* magazine called "the most diverse square mile in the nation." She is mom to four sons and three of their wives. She's Kiki (a much cooler name for Grandmother, almost as cool as her husband's Grandfather name, Chief) to a growing tribe of grandkids. She is a voracious reader, slow distance runner, killer cappuccino maker, and storyteller for hire. Kitti loves to show off God's mighty love and tender mercy by writing about the exploits of modern-day kingdom heroes. You can find her at kittimurray.com

Fazal Family Album

Young love: Mom and Dad

THE AWKWARD YEARS: Obea, Mahmood, Atiya, me, and Ali

THE ORIGINALS: Atiya, Ali, Moody, Me, Obea, Mom, and Dad

233

The fantastic five: Ali, Me, Atiya, Moody, and Obea

THE PRETTY ONES: Obea, Balques (mom), and Atiya

Two nerds:
me and Moody;
(bottom) Several
years later, two
cool nerds: me
and Moody

Loving life: Nurah, Asher, Ashley, and me